— 15,000

Seven Years
to
Seven Figures

The Fast-Track Plan
to Becoming a Millionaire

MICHAEL MASTERSON

WILEY

John Wiley & Sons, Inc.

Published by John Wiley & Sons, Inc., Hoboken, New Jersey
Published simultaneously in Canada

For general information about our other products and services, please contact our Customer Care Department within the United States at 800-762-2974, outside the United States at 317-572-3993 or fax 317-572-4002.

Wiley also publishes its books in a variety of electronic formats. Some content that appears in print may not be available in electronic books. For more information about Wiley products, visit our web site at www.wiley.com.

Library of Congress Cataloging-in-Publication Data:
Masterson, Michael.
    Seven years to seven figures : the fast-track plan to becoming a millionaire / Michael Masterson.
        p. cm.
    ISBN-13: 978-0-471-78675-7 (cloth)
    ISBN-10: 0-471-78675-6 (cloth)
    1. Wealth—United States.   2. Millionaires—United States—Case studies.
    3. Success in business.   4. Finance, Personal.   I. Title.
    HC110.W4M375 2006
332.024'01—dc22   2006024005

Printed in the United States of America

10 9 8 7 6 5 4 3 2 1

CONTENTS

ACKNOWLEDGMENTS

First, I want to thank Suzanne Richardson, an extremely bright and capable young woman who worked as my assistant on this book. Suzanne did a good deal of the research and all of the interviews.

None of my writing would be readable were it not for the intelligent edifications of Judith Strauss. Judith has been my editor longer than either of us would care to admit. I wouldn't feel comfortable publishing anything that hadn't been trimmed and polished by her.

I want to say special thank yous to Charlie Byrne, editorial director of my e-zine *Early to Rise*, and Steve Sjuggerud, editor of *True Wealth*, whose insightful and experienced comments helped me identify which, of the many ideas I initially wrote down, were important and worth keeping. Thanks also to Dave Lashmet and Gary Lundberg, whose financial expertise was invaluable in reviewing, correcting, and updating the financial planning portions of this book.

The folks in Agora Inc.'s book publishing department—Michael Ward, Wayne Ellis, and Danielle Morino—were, as usual, extraordinarily patient and helpful in working with the John Wiley team. In particular, I'd like to thank Joan O'Neil, my publisher, for her faith in the book and willingness to make last-minute changes.

And, finally, my admiration and gratitude go out to all of those people who inspired this book and whose wealth-building ideas, strategies, and techniques deepened and extended my own: Audrey Maxwell, Alan Silver, Bruce Buffer, Justin Ford, Ken Morris, Monica Day, David Keller, and Brad Solomon, I thank you.

FOREWORD

I haven't hit 35 yet, but . . .

By the time you read this book, my million-dollar-plus Florida home 100 steps from the ocean will be fully paid for. And I'll be debt free, with plenty of investments in other things as well, thanks in part to the author of this book. As he's done for so many others, he taught me how to do the right things to dramatically increase my income and net worth. Life is good.

It wasn't always like this . . .

When I was 23, I had zero net worth and a $23,500 a year salary. I went looking for something better, and met Michael Masterson on a job interview. I took a position with a company he consulted with.

Soon after that, I started using Michael's techniques and strategies to build my wealth. I knew he had succeeded (and failed) in many businesses over the years—and, watching him, I saw that he really analyzes every detail of what it takes to "make it." As a shortcut to success, I thought I could use what he'd learned so I could avoid mistakes and do the right things.

Following his lead, the changes in my financial situation were almost immediate. I knew exactly what to do to get ahead in my job, and I was doing it.

And the benefits have compounded every year. In fact, my net worth has probably increased tenfold in the last five years—during a time when the stock market's done nothing.

I credit Michael with getting me on track. I'm still influenced by him today—and not only in terms of wealth building. Michael has spent more time thinking about how to live a life that's rich in every way than anyone I know.

For example, he recommends starting each year by setting one significant goal for each of four important areas of your life: your health, your wealth, your personal self, and your social self. He says to make each goal "significant, yet specific." Once again, I've followed his advice . . .

On the last day of the year, I set significant, specific goals. And to keep myself honest, I share them with the more than 100,000 subscribers to my *True Wealth* newsletter. So far, I've followed through with all of them, and I've accomplished things I never imagined I could.

To succeed, of course, you have to put out some real effort. It will take your personal commitment, not just reading Michael's suggestions. But I can tell you from my own experience, he knows exactly what it takes to get you there. He's done it himself, time and again.

Seven Years to Seven Figures sounds like a tall order (unless, of course, you're starting with eight figures). But with Michael Masterson, you couldn't be in better hands.

Steve Sjuggerud
June 30, 2006

INTRODUCTION

SEVEN YEARS TO FINANCIAL INDEPENDENCE

This is a book about how to create your own, personal retirement fund before it is too late to enjoy it.

In the bulk of this book, I'll profile people who have followed that recommendation. These are real stories about people I've known, worked with, and admired. By reading their stories, you will be able to identify means and methods of increasing your own income and boosting the returns you are getting on your investments. Then, seven years from the time you begin your program to take charge of your future, you too can enjoy the comfort that financial independence brings.

Note: All the success stories in this book are true. Where the individual has requested that we use a pseudonym, the name is marked with an asterisk (*).

HOW LONG ARE YOU WILLING TO WAIT TO GET RICH?

So . . . how long are you willing to wait?

Whenever I ask this question—at dinner parties or seminars—I get the same answers.

Almost no one is willing to wait 40 years. Or 30 years, for that matter. The last time I asked this question at a conference—to an audience of about 350 people—I don't think a single hand went up at 40 years or 30 years. When I asked how many were willing to wait 20 years to get rich, three or four hands went up. It was not until I brought the goal closer to the present—to the 10-year mark—that a significant portion of the audience responded.

Not surprisingly, I have discovered that most people want to get rich as fast as possible and are "willing to wait" about seven years.

When I reported this finding to my publisher last year, he suggested I write a book about how to become wealthy in seven years. And when I suggested that idea to a marketing group that was doing an audiotape version of *Automatic Wealth* (the book that contains most of my best ideas on wealth building), the idea of writing something called *Seven Years to Seven Figures* was proposed.

I'm not sure who came up with that title. It may have been me. But I remember thinking about it after we'd all agreed to go ahead with the project. And I remember that I felt very uncomfortable. A program that can deliver a million-dollar fortune in seven years or less?

I worried that I had gotten myself into a bad situation by agreeing to accomplish a seemingly impossible goal. But the more I thought about it, the more I realized that I knew how to do it. After all, I had done it myself.

In *Automatic Wealth*, I outlined what I believe to be a realistic program for achieving financial independence. It's a balanced system that is based on a multi-tiered approach:

- Increasing your income
- Saving most of that extra money
- Investing it in a combination of real estate, stocks, and bonds
- Using your spare time (and some of your spare money) to start your own business

This system differs from most pinch-save-and-wait programs in that it recognizes an important truth: to get rich in less than 40 years, you have to radically increase your income.

In *Automatic Wealth*, my recommended method for increasing income involves real estate and entrepreneurship. If you are interested in a comprehensive wealth-building program that really works over a period of, say, 10 to 20 years, I recommend that book to you.

But if you can't (or don't want to) wait 10 or 20 years, you are reading the right book right now. Because the program that is laid out here is a proven, practical, completely realistic way of acquiring a seven-figure net worth in seven years or less.

It's not easy. And it's not guaranteed. But it works.

The program I'm suggesting here—the *Seven Years to Seven Figures* program—is based on the principles explained in *Automatic Wealth* . . . but modified to achieve a multimillion-dollar net worth in far less time.

Think of it as *Automatic Wealth* on steroids.

As I said, when I first began working on this concept of accelerated wealth, I was afraid I couldn't do it. But when I thought about how long it took me to make each of the million-dollar fortunes I've earned, I realized that none of them took longer than seven years. Most of them, in fact, took three or four years. This is something to keep in mind as you read this book: the strategies I suggest—though designed to work for you in seven years—may do better than that.

THIS BOOK IS NOT JUST FOR BABY BOOMERS

The idea for this book came to me as the result of many conversations I've had about wealth with all sorts of people. Many of them were middle-aged and thus needed an accelerated wealth-building program so they could retire while they were still relatively young.

But many were younger people—people who planned to work another 20 or 30 or even another 40 years, but didn't want to wait that long to become wealthy.

The truth is, it doesn't matter how old you are. The principles and strategies (as well as the stories) presented in the following pages will help you learn how to become rich in seven years.

INTRODUCING THE *SEVEN YEARS TO SEVEN FIGURES* PROGRAM

Getting rich involves three components:

- How *long* you invest
- How *much* you invest
- What *rate of return* you achieve on your investments

How *long* you will invest has already been figured out: seven years.

How *much* you will invest is largely dependent on your income. Pinch-save-and-wait programs are based on making small investments, which means they are based on the assumption that you aren't going to have a high income.

Theoretically, you can become wealthy by increasing any one of these three components. And so, theoretically, you could develop a seven-figure income in seven years just by getting a very high rate of return on a modest investment.

For example, let's assume you and your spouse have a combined income of $70,000 a year (which is actually about $9,500 above the average). If you saved 10 percent of that, or $7,000 each year, it would take a return on investment (ROI) of 82 percent to reach a million dollars in seven years.

There is no investment I know that can give you that sort of return.

Most financial planners will tell you that you can't reliably achieve more than a 6 percent or 8 percent ROI over any length of time. As I'll explain a bit later, I think that's ridiculous.

But even if you calculate in the higher ROIs that I believe are possible using this program, your average rate of return on your savings will still be in the 15 percent to 20 percent range—hardly enough to turn $7,000 into a million in seven years.

To achieve a seven-figure net worth in seven years, it helps to get a higher ROI . . . but it is absolutely necessary to *radically increase your income*.

This book will help you do just that. But before we look at the way others have done it, I'd like to tell you my own story.

PART I

SEVEN YEARS TO SEVEN FIGURES: IS IT REALLY POSSIBLE?

I've broken this book into three parts so you can use it efficiently. Here's what you'll find:

In Part I, I make my case: that you can't get rich quickly by following most of the advice you get from newspapers, television, booksellers, and the Internet. Such popular advice is all about passive investing. My experience (and the lessons I've learned from friends and colleagues who've made money quickly) suggests a different course of action.

Part II presents eight inspiring stories–step-by-step accounts of the successes of eight people I know personally. Read them once for motivation. Read them a second time for specific strategies and techniques you can use to build your own wealth.

If you're a baby boomer nearing retirement–or someone younger who simply doesn't want to wait 40 years to get rich—you'll have a particular interest in Part III, which explains why the *Seven Years to Seven Figures* program is perfect for you.

Get ready to begin your path to seven figures. . . .

CHAPTER 1

WHAT THE HECK DO I KNOW?

This book is all about creating a seven-figure net worth in seven years or less. That may sound outrageous . . . even impossible. But it can be done. In fact, I've done it many times.

It started in 1983, when I first decided to get rich.

I was taking a 14-week Dale Carnegie course. Each week, we were given a challenge—to learn how to give a good "hello," to refrain from criticism . . . that kind of thing. We would read what Dale Carnegie said about the subject in his book *How to Win Friends and Influence People*, figure out how we intended to implement that lesson in our lives, come into class and explain to everyone there what we specifically aimed to do—and then, the following week and for the rest of the course, we would practice that skill and report back to the class on our progress.

The lesson for week four was about priorities. Our challenge was to identify our 10 top goals, narrow them to five, narrow them again to three, and finally pick one as our primary goal.

In his book, Carnegie said something that had a profound impact on me. He said that while it is true that *most* people don't succeed because they don't have clearly defined goals, *some* people fail to make progress because they have too many.

He was right. That was my problem. If you have many goals—as I did—you can't achieve them all. If you don't narrow them down and prioritize them, you may achieve none of them. I realized that for ambitious people like me (and maybe you, too), establishing priorities is a critical first step toward achieving anything.

So I got to work on our assignment for the week.

It was easy to narrow my many goals to 10, but thinning out the list even further was tough. At the time, I had a decent job as editorial director for a fledgling business-newsletter publisher in south Florida, but I wanted—*really* wanted—to be many things. I wanted to be a novelist, a humanitarian, a teacher, a black belt, a philosopher, a poet, a perfect specimen of physical health and fitness. And, yes, I wanted to be rich, too. (Though, being a child of Woodstock and a former Peace Corps volunteer, I was a little embarrassed by my monetary desires.)

It took me a couple of days to get that list down to five. Getting to three was excruciating, but I managed to do it the day before I was due to announce my number one goal in class. I had 24 hours to choose among my favorite three: writer, teacher, and (my noblest ambition) humanitarian.

The task proved to be almost impossible. In fact, this final cut was so difficult that I was still undecided as I walked into class. And it wasn't until I was actually walking up to the podium that it came to me.

I thought to myself, "Hmm . . . writer, teacher, humanitarian . . . rich guy . . .

"Rich guy! Right! And if I'm not happy with the money, I can always give it away. That would make me a humanitarian!"

HOW TO MAKE DECISIONS THAT STICK

It was a last-minute, illogical, and cowardly decision, but it turned out to be one of the most important decisions I've ever made. It changed my life. It led directly to my becoming wealthy. And it eventually proved to me that I could do just about anything I wanted to do.

This wasn't the first time I had identified a top-of-the-list goal for myself. I had done it plenty of times before. In fact, my longest-standing goal—to become a professional writer—had been at or near the top of my list of "wants" for as long as I could remember, it was a perennial New Year's resolution.

But, as Dale Carnegie said, making a decision to achieve a goal won't do you any good if you have already decided to achieve a dozen other goals.

After we announced our top priority in class, we were told that we had to spend the remaining 10 weeks of the course focusing on it. At the beginning of every day, we had to remind ourselves that we had a purpose. And throughout the day, we had to make sure that all our actions and decisions reflected that purpose.

Dale Carnegie argued—and I've come to believe he was 100 percent correct—that the best way to guarantee that you will accomplish an objective is to make it your number one priority. The combination of making "getting rich" my top priority and focusing on it for 10 straight weeks made a huge difference. In retrospect, it sounds like a commonsense strategy—but to me, at the time, it was revolutionary.

All of a sudden, I was thinking differently at work. Before, when challenged by business problems, I was sometimes unsure about which direction to take. Choices were complicated. Decisions were difficult. I had no way of cutting through the maze, because I didn't have a final objective against which I could measure my options. But once I had "getting rich" as a priority, much of the confusion evaporated. All I had to do was ask myself, "Which choice will result in making me richer?"

I don't mean to imply that I ignored other important considerations (like the editorial quality of our publications, customer satisfaction, etc.). I didn't. But I was no longer stymied by them, either. I'd first figure out which option would result in greater profits for the company (and thus more income for me) . . . and then I'd weigh the other issues accordingly.

Often, I opted to take a course that would result in less profit but more quality (sometimes simply because I felt a moral imperative for quality). Even then, having my number one priority firmly in place made those decisions easier.

ANATOMY OF A REALLY BIG RAISE

Driving to work the day after I made that momentous decision to get rich, I realized that there was no way I was going to do it by gradually working my way up the corporate ladder. I was making $35,000 at the time. So, even assuming I would get above-average salary increases, there was no way I'd be enjoying the million-dollar lifestyle I wanted in a timeframe that was acceptable to me.

I had to drastically increase my income. And since my only income at the time was my salary, it was crystal clear to me that I had to transform myself. I could no longer afford to be an editorial taskmaster. I had to somehow become my company's top employee.

Prior to making that decision, I had been spending lots of my time fussing with the company's editors, trying to get them to write better. "Better" to me meant writing the way my college English professors had taught me to write. But now that I had this clear focus—on getting rich—I realized instantly that I had been wasting my time. Ninety-eight percent of the people reading our newsletters didn't care about the stylistics or grammar. What they cared about were exciting, money-making ideas.

If I wanted to help my company grow, I had to forget about Strunk & White and the *Chicago Manual of Style* and focus on how to find more and better opportunities for our subscribers.

So that's what I did. In doing so, I realized that the growth of the company would depend on the direct-mail efforts made by our marketing department to attract new customers and keep old ones. I didn't know anything about that side of the business, but I committed to learning all about it. I read everything I could lay my hands on—including the marketing classics written by David Ogilvy, Claude Hopkins, John Caples, and Eugene Schwartz. Based on what I read, I started asking questions. How many pieces are we mailing? What elements are we testing? Why didn't we include a business reply envelope in that package?

Just by asking those kinds of questions, I was letting the higher-ups in the company know that I wanted to advance. This was appreciated by some . . . but the director of marketing didn't like it. She thought I should stick to the editorial side of the business. I could understand her point of view and would have acceded to her request . . . except for one thing: I had made myself that promise to get wealthy.

DON'T BE AFRAID OF YOUR UNDERLINGS

I assured her that I had no intentions of stealing her job. I told her that I wanted to help her succeed by dovetailing editorial and marketing. If she had the same commitment to the company's future that I had, she would have recognized in me a great ally. But instead she looked at me as an enemy.

The more I learned about marketing, the less she liked me. She eventually ended up devoting an insane amount of her time to trying to get me fired. She would get her husband, a writer, to criticize the editorial work I had done, and she would relay those criticisms to the owner of the company. He would call me in, and she would repeat the charges. I would defend myself, and, since she knew nothing about writing or editing, she couldn't refute me. In fact, a few of her husband's criticisms might have made sense, but she wasn't able to make a convincing argument for them. The end result of all those encounters was bad for her. She was embarrassing herself in front of the one person in the company she should have been trying to please.

She should have retreated and let me do my thing, but she persisted. Finally, she gave the boss an ultimatum: "It's him or me," she said. Bad career move.

A month later, I was up for a review. The boss was so pleased with my progress, he gave me the biggest raise he'd ever given anyone: from $35,000 to $55,000.

It was a generous raise, and I was grateful to him for it. But because I had made getting wealthy my number one priority, I had to say, "Thanks. It's great. But I need more."

He looked at me, shocked.

"But you don't deserve more," he said.

"I know," I admitted. "But if you give me more I'll make myself worth it. I'll find a way to pay you back a hundredfold by making the business much more profitable."

He said, "Let me think about it overnight." The next morning, I was making $70,000.

BECOMING A CHICKEN ENTREPRENEUR

Six months later, I was working two jobs: heading up the editorial group and editing promotions for the marketing department. My boss decided not to replace the departed director. Instead, he was going to teach me what he knew about selling (which was considerable).

Neither of us was an expert in direct-mail marketing, but he was confident we could figure it out.

I applied the ideas I had read about, and he provided the wisdom he'd accumulated from 20 years of being in business. We also spent some time studying the promotions of our most successful competitors. Piece by piece, we were able to figure out why most of the packages we were mailing weren't doing very well and how to create new ones that did better. Month by month, our little publishing business went from losing $15,000 a month to making about that much.

A year later, I was ready to test myself against the competition. I decided to create my own product and sell it using my own direct-mail package. I had been studying the investment advisory market for some time, and had an idea for a new and better type of financial newsletter.

Working at home at night and on weekends, I outlined the project, created the product, wrote the editorial copy, wrote the promotion, made contacts, and so on.

When it was ready, I went to my boss and told him that I had invented an entirely new type of newsletter, that I had written a promotion for it, and I was hoping that, if he liked it, he would let me take "a piece of the action."

"You're an employee," he said. "What makes you think I should give you a piece of this thing?"

"I did it on my own time," I told him.

"As far as I'm concerned," he said, "all your time is mine."

I argued that the product itself was completely new and different. He shrugged his shoulders.

Finally, I said that I knew I couldn't expect him to give me huge salary increases every six months . . . so I figured getting a piece of a product was a good way for me to get what I wanted without taking anything out of his pocket.

That seemed to make sense to him. Once again, he said he'd think about it overnight. And once again, when I arrived at work the next morning, I was a richer man.

Not richer immediately. The promotion I wrote for my newsletter—thanks to all the help he gave me to improve it—was a big hit. But as I was about to learn, success is expensive. To bring the circulation of that newsletter up to where it needed to be that first year was going to cost us about $2 million in marketing expenses.

My boss made me mortgage the little bit of equity I had in my starter home and car to support my 25 percent stake. By forcing me to risk the only money I had, he taught me a lesson about the value of money.

My debt was up to almost half a million dollars when the cash flow of the newsletter started to turn around. I remember the first day we had a positive bottom line. My share of that day's profits was $7,000! I went home and told my wife that we had made an extra $7,000 that day . . . and that I didn't do any extra work to get it.

"That's the value of equity," I told her. A year later, my stake in the newsletter was worth about $1.5 million.

That entire process—from deciding I wanted to become rich to becoming a millionaire—took less than two years.

BUT THAT WAS JUST THE BEGINNING

In the 10 years that followed my first million-dollar venture, I started or co-started at least 50 separate and distinct businesses. Everything from resale to wholesale to manufacturing to import-export to information publishing and various services.

I was also involved in just about every form of marketing, including direct sales, direct marketing, television commercials, magazine advertising, point-of-purchase promotions, radio advertising, and Internet-based promotions.

I sold houses, cars, office furniture, televisions, watches, perfume, costume jewelry, magazines, newsletters, special reports, books, seminars, conferences, trade shows, nutritional products, promotional gimmicks, club memberships—you name it.

In the beginning, most of my attempts failed. As I gained experience, my batting average improved. Eventually, my track record for successful launches was about 70 percent. And at least half of the successful launches I was involved in became multimillion-dollar-makers.

Some of those businesses lasted only a few years. Others have been alive and kicking for decades. (One of them grew into a highly profitable $20 million business that is still going strong 20 years later.)

From each of them, I earned a good deal of money . . . and most of that money went into savings. What I did with those savings made me very wealthy. Looking back at the many successes I enjoyed during that period of time (from 1981 to 1992), I can honestly say that none of the two dozen (or so) fortunes I made took more than seven years to achieve. The vast majority, in fact, were made in around three years.

In 1992, I retired from business for 18 months. During that time, I wrote dozens of short stories and published 12. Of those that were published, two won literary prizes. But my total compensation for all the work I did during that 18-month period (apart from the considerable gratification of winning those awards) was only about $875.

In 1993, I went back into business with a former competitor. His business was doing about $25 million in sales, but it had no profits. Our mutually agreed upon goal was to increase the profits as soon as possible. Within 12 months, we had earned our first million dollars.

In the 13 years that have transpired since then, that business has grown substantially. Today, revenues are in excess of $200 million, and profits are through the roof.

When I started my business career for the second time, there were plenty of things I wanted to do differently. For one thing, I didn't want to sell "stuff." What I wanted to do was sell good ideas. And the company I went to work for was chock-full of brainy, idea-oriented people.

My second business career has demanded all sorts of different skills and habits, and I happily developed them. During the last 13 years, I have started or co-started dozens of businesses within the context of this company, and almost every one of them hit the million-dollar mark in four years or less.

I have learned from my successes and from my failures. And what I didn't learn from my own experiences, I learned from the experiences of people I know. I've passed it all on to friends and colleagues who have become wealthy by following in my footsteps. (Some of them are now even wealthier than I am.)

And now, I pass it on to you . . .

When it comes to building a seven-figure fortune, seven years is not a long time to wait. Time passes regardless of what you do. So why not spend the next seven years getting wealthy?

You have a choice. You can read this book and follow the plan, or you can put it down and click on the television. You can do that today. And you can do that tomorrow. Watching television is the easier choice. But it's not likely to help you achieve your goals.

If you decide to put down this book and watch the boob tube instead, you'll almost assuredly wake up one day and ask yourself, "Whatever happened to my idea of becoming a millionaire before I was [fill in the blank] years old?"

If you really want to know what it feels like to be financially independent—to be able to quit working while still enjoying a comfortable lifestyle (and with plenty of "go-to-hell" money in your pocket)—follow the suggestions you will find in *Seven Years to Seven Figures*.

Remember, there is nothing in this book—not one piece of advice or specific recommendation—that hasn't already worked for me or someone I know.

CHAPTER 2

ARE YOU READY
FOR WEALTH?

Compound interest is an amazing thing, but waiting for your compounded savings to reach seven figures can take decades . . . even if you're getting excellent returns. That's why I'm not recommending a pinch-save-and-wait wealth program. Why? Because inflation, taxes, and time make it hard to build a fortune. Yes, those programs work well for college graduates and other young people who are just starting out, but they make no sense for baby boomers or anyone who doesn't want to scrape and save for 40 years.

In Chapter 1, I told you that when I was first considering the idea for *Seven Years to Seven Figures* I realized just about every million-dollar fortune I've made in my career was accomplished in fewer than seven years. That's true for all of my mentors, as well as most of the people I've mentored.

You have already heard my story. Now I'm going to tell you a little about *their* success.

Before we begin, I'd like you to spend a few moments contemplating a fundamental truth about wealth. This may already be obvious to you. But it wasn't always obvious to me—and it wasn't until I truly understood it that I was ready and willing to become wealthy.

The truth is this: some forms of wealth are limited. Others can be recreated. Natural resources (coal, oil, natural gas, etc.) are available in limited supply. Human resources (intelligence, creativity, and skill) are available in infinite quantities.

Most of the products of intelligence, creativity, and skill are also unlimited. As long as there are 100 people living on this planet, there will be 100,000 possibilities for creating wealth.

A hundred years ago, there were horses and buggies, telegraphs and steamships. Now there are cell phones, three-car garages, and jumbo jets. There are washing machines and refrigerators. Antibiotics and polio vaccines. TVs and satellites and MRI machines.

All this technology was invented, and it has not only enriched our world but has also made more than a few people wealthy.

Here's another example, much closer to home. My house was built 10 years ago. It replaced a smaller house, built in the 1960s. Before that house, this spot was an empty bit of beach. Something—a very nice house—replaced nothing. That makes my little piece of real estate part of a vast and growing economy.

See what I'm saying? Wealth—whether in the form of technology, ideas, or property—is created all the time.

Let's see how that applies to the way my two main mentors built their fortunes . . .

PERRY WAGNER*

Perry Wagner, my first boss in the publishing business, was a German war orphan who saw his parents shot down on the street. Perry came to America, got himself enrolled in the Ivy League, and—though he never excelled at academics—went on to make a fortune selling International Harvester equipment to the Russians during the height of the Cold War. "You'll never make any money in the USSR," his classmates told him. But he did.

Despite all the difficulties of doing business with the USSR at the time, Perry pushed through the red tape and prejudice and convinced International Harvester to let him "try" to sell their tractors to the Soviets. Back then, he told me, there were so many obstacles in the way of doing business with Eastern bloc countries that most large companies simply didn't try. But Perry never doubted that he would eventually be successful. "Sooner or later," he said, "I knew I could convince everyone that it was in their own best interests to do business."

And he did. Not on his first attempt. And not on his second. But about four trade-show trips, 22 months of investing, and 500 official forms later, Perry made a deal. He sold $10 million worth of tractors to one of the USSR's many state-run companies. His commission, as an independent agent in a tough market, was large. I think he said he received 10 percent.

Perry went on to sell agricultural equipment all over the world, and he became a wealthy man when he was still in his thirties. But his first fortune, the million-dollar paycheck he got from doing the impossible in Moscow, was made in less than two years.

Perry was the kind of guy I've called a *pusher* in my e-zine, *Early to Rise.* By that I mean someone who can *push* people into working harder than they want to, taking more risks than they feel comfortable with, being more creative than they believe they can be . . . and always doing better than they did the time before.

That's what he did with me when I worked for him. I was running one of his companies, a little publishing business that produced newsletters in the USSR, Africa, and Latin America. Perry had about a half-dozen companies that did business in those areas. He didn't know much about publishing—and didn't especially care to know—but he understood sales. Every day, he would ask me to show him how many checks came in. And every afternoon, he would ask me what I'd done to make sure more checks were coming in the next day.

Perry would force me to go to embassy functions with him (we were situated in Washington, D.C.) and help him pass out our newsletters to everyone in the room. "Nice to see you, Mr. Ambassador," he would say, introducing me. Then, "Michael, give him a newsletter. Good. Now Mr. Ambassador, your embassy should subscribe to this service."

Perry didn't have a superego. There was something missing in his psyche—the part that would normally keep a person from overreaching. But this gave him the guts to be a sort of genius when it came to selling. He was not embarrassed to ask and then ask again and then ask again and again and again until, finally, he got the answer he was looking for.

Once, when I ruined a company car by running it without oil, he had me call the manufacturer at least 500 times to insist that they replace the out-of-warranty engine for free. Even after the vice president of Honda Motors called to personally tell us they couldn't do it—and beg us to stop badgering them—Perry had me call him back to give it one more try. I don't have to tell you what happened, do I? We got a new car.

JOHN NEWMAN*

John Newman was my greatest business mentor. He had Perry's tenacity and a brilliant mind—one of the strongest business minds I've ever encountered. John taught me many things about doing business, the first and most important being why *making money fast* is critical to long-term success.

I began my career with John as editorial director of the group of business newsletters I told you about in Chapter 1. In the beginning, most of our titles had a very limited appeal—like *Robotics Update* and *Agribusiness Review.* The business was funded by people who neither knew nor cared much about newsletter publishing. They didn't even care if we made a profit, because a loss made a nice tax write-off for them.

But John did care about making a profit. And it was clear to him that most of what I was doing as editorial director was not going to have that result.

"Let me ask you something," John said to me after he'd been observing me for about a month. "What do you think your job is?"

I wasn't sure what he meant.

"I mean, why do you think I hired you? What do you think I expect you to do?"

"I think you hired me to improve the editorial quality of your newsletters."

"I did. But how do you define 'quality'?"

I went into a rambling dissertation. He listened for a while, and then cut me off.

"I don't pretend to know anything about writing or about newsletters," he admitted. "But I do know a good deal about business. The first and most important thing a business has to do is make sales. And every person in the business must define his role accordingly."

"Which means?" I wanted to know.

"Which means I'm going to give you a simple definition of editorial quality. It's whatever makes it easier for us to sell these damn newsletters. In other words, whatever kind of writing brings in the most money the fastest."

I was, of course, outraged and indignant to even think that I would devote my precious talents to something so . . . so . . . commercially tacky. But this was right about the time that I decided I wanted to become wealthy. (See Chapter 1.) And the moment I made that decision, I understood that in some profound way John was absolutely right.

When I decided I wanted to become wealthy, I realized that I had to help make this newsletter publishing company very successful. If not, then how could I expect to get big raises?

Within days of my big decision, I had totally revamped our editorial guidelines. Instead of opinions that were clever and intelligent, I demanded copy that was useful and clear. Instead of language that was dense and ironic, I insisted on simple, readable English.

The titles of our publications changed, too. Instead of newsletters on arcane industries that had a limited market, we began publishing investment newsletters with more mainstream appeal. "Let your subscribers tell you what to write about," John wisely advised me. "Don't try to outsmart the market."

Before I had my "conversion," our little business was in the red. But when we started to work together toward that common, profit-making goal, things really moved. "If you don't know what to do in business," he once said, "ask yourself a simple question: 'What will make the most money?'" As I've already explained, I quickly came to see the logic and value of this approach.

John was not an editor but he was a moneymaking genius. By instinctively orienting himself toward the money, he was able to do things that most of his colleagues and competitors couldn't do. It was this simple trait, I'm convinced, that allowed him to build three multimillion-dollar businesses before he got into publishing. And it was this, plus the experience of those three businesses, that made him such a great leader in our business.

As smart a guy as John is, his thought processes were relatively simple when it came to business decisions: business is about profit. And profit is good. Adapting this simple thinking to my own knowledge and experience helped both of us create a multimillion-dollar business in two years that turned into a $135 million business seven years later.

TAKE YOUR FIRST STEP TOWARD FINANCIAL INDEPENDENCE . . . RIGHT NOW

The first step on my own road to wealth began with a promise—the promise I made to myself on that fateful day when I decided to get rich. And that's something you can do right now. Make yourself a promise that getting wealthy is going to be your top priority.

By top priority, I mean *top* priority.

One of the fundamental principles I write about in *Early to Rise* is the importance of having a full, balanced life—one that includes not only work but also friends, family, and community involvement. That means you should think in terms of four categories when setting goals:

- Your health
- Your wealth
- Your social life
- Your personal life

Seven years from now, for example, you might want to have:

- Attained and maintained your high school body weight
- Achieved a seven-figure net worth
- Become your town's mayor
- Written and published your first novel

These are all reachable goals, but they are also ambitious. If you give them equal weight, chances are you will not be entirely successful. You might become mayor, and maybe even get down to that perfect body weight . . . but you'll more than likely be struggling with the novel and disappointed by your wealth-building accomplishments.

There's only one way to be absolutely sure that you'll reach your financial goal (having a seven-figure net worth in seven years): you have to make it your top priority. That is, you have to elevate it to the status of *first among equals.* Yes, your other three main goals are extremely important to you, but wealth building always has to come first—every year, every month, every week, and even every day.

If you aren't willing to make *seven years to seven figures* your top priority, you can still benefit greatly from the program in this book . . . but your chances of hitting your financial target will be diminished.

How much so? I can't say for sure, but significantly. Making something your absolute top priority is a life-changing event. If you can't

---

THE PARABLE OF THE PROFESSOR AND THE BUCKET

A philosophy professor and his student stand in a warehouse. A large tin bucket and several boxes of stones and sand are in front of them.

The professor picks up a box that contains large rocks, each one about four inches in diameter, and pours them into the bucket. The stones reach the top of the bucket, and he asks the student if it is full.

"It is," the student replies.

The professor takes another box, this one containing stones about one inch in diameter, and pours them over the rocks in the bucket. The smaller stones fill in the spaces between the rocks. Again, he asks the student if the bucket is full.

The student looks and says, "It is."

The professor then pours in the contents of a third box, this one containing small pebbles. Again, the student looks in the bucket and agrees that it is full.

Finally, the professor pours a box of sand on top of the rocks, stones, and pebbles—and once more, for the fourth time, the student has to acknowledge that the bucket is full.

"Do the most important things first," the professor advises the student, "and each lesser thing in order of its priority. In this way, you will be able to fill up your life four times, instead of just once. If you do the unimportant things first, you'll be filling your bucket with sand . . . and there won't be room for anything else."

or won't do that with your financial objective, you must face the fact that you may not succeed at it.

I should back up here to point this out: making the achievement of seven figures in seven years your top priority doesn't mean you will neglect your other goals. But it does mean you will limit the time and attention you give to them.

Right now, for example, my top priority is writing fiction. Every morning, after stretching and showering, I grab a cup of coffee, cross the courtyard that separates my house from the garage, and climb the spiral staircase that leads to my writing room. Beginning at six thirty or seven, I work away at my novel. I work diligently until nine o'clock sharp. Then I pack up my briefcase and drive to the office.

The time I spend writing fiction is limited. Two and a half hours in the morning, at most. And yet, I am moving my number one goal forward every day. As a result, my chances of finishing this novel—a dream I've had for most of my adult life—are nearly 100 percent certain.

Getting wealthier is no longer a goal for me. My net worth is already more than I will ever need. I continue to set business goals for myself, but none of them are related to making money. (Most have to do with making sure that businesses I started continue to flourish.) I've found that since I stopped caring about making money, I'm making as much as I ever did. Still, I wouldn't advise someone who was just starting out on the path to wealth to do what I'm doing now. I got rich by making wealth building my top priority. If you want to achieve your wealth-building goal, I'd feel honor-bound to recommend that you do the same.

Let's assume that you are willing to make wealth building your top priority and that you recognize this means devoting the first hour or two of every day to the specific suggestions outlined in this book. Let's get started with the program by figuring out how much wealth is right for you.

WHEN IT COMES TO WEALTH, HOW MUCH IS ENOUGH?

Seven figures means, literally, $1 million to $9 million. For the purposes of this book, *net worth* means the total of all your assets minus all your debts. So a seven-figure net worth means that if you sold everything you had and then paid off all your debts, the wealth you'd have left would be between $1 million and $9 million.

Let's take a look at the impact of having that kind of wealth. I've put together a few "lifestyle budgets" to show you how life would "feel" at several seven-figure net worth levels.

The purpose is to help you choose a specific goal for yourself—and, hopefully, help you realize that you may not need as much money as you think.

Of course, when you are setting wealth-building goals at the age of 40 or 50, you have to be realistic. Creating a $9 million net worth in seven years is harder than achieving a million dollars of wealth. It's not nine times harder, but it's harder.

My wealth is considerably higher than seven figures. Why I didn't stop when I hit that number, I can't really say. I do know that I fell into a very common trap—thinking that what I had was good, but not quite enough. That's the danger of creating personal wealth. The process itself can become addictive. If you are not careful, you get fixated on the numbers. The more you have, the more you think you need.

I read somewhere that if you ask wealthy people how much money they need to feel comfortable, they will almost always choose a number that is twice what they have. The man who has a $2 million net worth will say $4 million. The woman who has achieved a net worth of $25 million will say $50 million.

You don't want to fall into that way of thinking. By picking a specific target now, and understanding what that target means in terms of lifestyle, you may be able to avoid it.

I know what you are thinking: "This is a problem I'd like to have." Trust me. Getting wealthy is not such a big accomplishment. Being content with your wealth—that takes some doing.

Now, let's figure out how rich you are going to be. Seven figures, as I said, means $1 million to $9 million. That's a pretty big range . . . too big to be useful as a target. Studies show that people who set specific goals have the greatest chance of achieving them. So let's make your seven-figure goal more specific. Let's pick a number—a nice, round, seven-figure number between $1 million and $9 million.

FOUR LEVELS OF SEVEN-FIGURE WEALTH

To help you make the choice, let's narrow down your choices to four:

- $1 million
- $2.5 million
- $5.5 million
- $9 million

As you'll see from the following scenarios, each of these levels will give you a different lifestyle. You may find that you'd be content with a fortune of $2.5 million or even less. If you can be happy with a smaller number, you are better off because that objective will be easier to reach and maintain.

One final note before we compare the four seven-figure lifestyles: in figuring how much income each of these fortunes would provide, I

YOU CAN MAKE MONEY BY INVESTING RIGHT

I've said it before: I'm no expert in the stock market. And I've always been fairly conservative in my own investments. But I do believe in stock market investing—as long as you have reasonable expectations and you invest with discipline.

I have been in the investment publishing business for more than 20 years, and I've seen many people become wealthy from the stock market. But 95 percent of them became wealthy by selling stocks or by selling advice about stocks.

If you read the studies, the truth about stock investing is clear: it is very, very hard to make a profit. Most professional money managers fail to do as well as index funds. And most individual investors actually lose money on a net- and inflation-adjusted basis.

But some investors do very well. Warren Buffett—one of the world's richest men—is the primary example.

Besides Buffett, I am personally acquainted with a handful of investors who have beaten the market over a long period of time (or so they tell me). They all have the same advice about investing in stocks:

- Buy good, profitable companies.
- Buy them when they are relatively undervalued.

These rare "stock superstars" differ about the key question: When is the right time to sell?

Some of them use stop losses. "If the price drops significantly, it's the market's way of telling you that you were wrong about the company," they say.

Some of them hold stocks for the long term, regardless of the market. Rodney Dir did just that. He made two fortunes. The first was from the stock market. The second was by doing what I recommend in this book. Read his story and see what you think. Read it again after you've finished the book and you may have a different idea.

The year was 1996. The Internet was booming, and so was the need for additional hard drive storage on personal computers. Putting these two elements together, Rodney envisioned that people were going to need massive amounts of portable memory in the future. And only one company could provide it: Iomega.

At the time, Iomega had great portable memory technology—but with the U.S. government as its primary customer, Iomega's sales and profits had been slowly eroding. Then it hired a marketing guru from GE to turn the company around. The new CEO took a boring government technology and made it into a sexy product to sell to consumers. The result: the ZIP drive.

When Rodney saw all this, he bought $10,000 worth of Iomega stock, and set his day job aside. All Rodney did was track Iomega's management, its products, its sales, and its profits. With this deep due diligence, he made over $700,000 on his initial investment. And along the way, he also bought more shares.

In 18 months, he banked over seven figures. Then he used the profits to start a brokerage firm to do the same kind of research for other investors. Today, Rodney's business continues to thrive using these same successful strategies.

Rodney also buys alternative investments like real estate, commodities, precious metals, and bonds. But his core path to seven figures was investing in small, growing businesses—and then building his own.

used 10 percent of the entire net worth number. Obviously, a considerable portion of your net worth—the part that is tied up in your home—will not be earning income. It should be appreciating (making you wealthier by becoming more valuable) but it won't give you an active income. The long-term stock market ROI (return on investment) has been 10 percent. But if you follow the income-accelerating methods outlined in this book, you'll be doing much better than that. You should do well enough that an overall 10 percent ROI, including the zero income you'll be getting from your house, will be your minimum average return.

More on that later. Right now, let's take a look at what it would feel like to be rich.

COPING WITH A MERE MILLION

To begin at the beginning, ask yourself: "Would a net worth of $1 million be enough for me?"

A million dollars earning 10 percent yields $100,000 in annual income. Take away about $35,000 for federal, state, and local taxes. That leaves you with $65,000 in cash. (The amount of tax you pay depends on where you live and what kind of deductions you have. If, for example, you incorporate your business and take the appropriate allowable deductions, $35,000 in taxes on a $100,000 income should be achievable.)

What kind of lifestyle would $65,000 buy?

Let's start with housing. You could spend a lot, but I've made it a rule to never spend more than 25 percent of my income on housing. (Today, I spend less than 2 percent . . . and your percentage will gradually diminish, too. But for the purpose of this example, I'm going to assume that you spend 25 percent of your active income on housing.)

Twenty-five percent of $65,000 is $16,250, or about $1,350 a month. What kind of housing would that give you?

In figuring housing costs, I always think in terms of rental costs, because the rental market is tied to what people can actually afford. So think about where you'd like to live once you achieve financial independence, and then ask yourself: "What kind of home could I rent in that neighborhood for $1,350 a month?"

(I am simplifying this analysis tremendously. If, for example, you own instead of rent, you'd have additional expenses but also tax deductions. For the purposes of planning, however, thinking in terms of rental costs is a reasonably reliable indicator of housing costs—apart from property appreciation—because rental costs are generally less than and seldom more than the cost of owning.)

If you did spend $1,350 a month on rent, you'd have about $4,000 left over to pay for other expenses. Utilities, upkeep, and routine maintenance on your home might be as much as 30 percent of your rental costs—that's $405. And you could expect to pay another $900 a month for food and household supplies. (These budgets are based on the presumption that you are a two-person family. If you want to get rich while the kids are still home, you'll have to make some adjustments.)

Transportation would be your next-biggest expense. Figure $600 a month for two medium-sized Toyotas.

Those are your major expenses. Do the math and you'll see that you are left with about $2,000 for things like travel, entertainment, dinners out, and other nonessentials. Those expenses can vary greatly, depending on your personal preferences. If you can be happy with a good meal at a local restaurant, you may be able to budget meals for two people at $80. If you prefer fancier places, you'll have to figure on spending two or three times that amount.

I am in the fortunate position of being able to pay whatever I want for restaurant meals—and I'm happy to tell you that although I do enjoy the occasional $500 meal, I'm usually just as happy eating meatballs and spaghetti at my local trattoria. Developing a plebeian palate will do a lot for your future happiness if your goal is to achieve a net worth of only $1 million.

THE $2.5 MILLION LIFESTYLE

Living on a nest egg of a million dollars could be completely satisfying . . . so long as you are content with modest choices. If you have a family that is larger than two people or if you want to be able to live on a somewhat higher level, you may want to target your net worth at $2 million or $3 million. For the purposes of this discussion, let's pick a number in between: $2.5 million.

What will a net worth of $2.5 million buy you? Again assuming a 10 percent ROI and a tax burden of 35 percent, you'd end up with disposable, after-tax income of about $160,000 a year.

And, again, figuring that 25 percent of that $160,000 will go into housing, ask yourself if you could be satisfied living in a house or apartment in your chosen neighborhood that would rent for about $40,000 a year or $3,300 a month.

In my neck of the woods—near the ocean in southeast Florida—that would get you a nice, older, two- or three-bedroom house within walking distance of town. If you want to live in Minneapolis, you'll do much better than that on the same budget. (Don't laugh. It's a great city.) On that kind of income, you can live there in a modern, spacious, six-bedroom house with all the bells and whistles.

Figuring, again, that you'd spend 30 percent of your housing budget on associated living expenses, you'd budget about $12,000 a year for utilities, repairs, maintenance, and upkeep. Other associated expenses—food, clothing, and so on—might account for another $13,000 a year, for a total of $25,000. That may seem a bit high, percentage-wise, as compared to the $1 million budget—but it's a financial fact of life that the more you pay for your home, the more you'll pay for living expenses.

Subtract the cost of housing ($40,000 a year) and associated living expenses ($25,000 a year), and you are left with about $95,000 to spend on luxuries.

Ninety-five thousand after-tax dollars a year will provide two people with a lot of extras. Just for fun, let's look at what a $95,000-lifestyle budget might buy:

10-day Hawaiian vacation for two:	$11,000
10-day London vacation for two:	$11,000
52 semi-fancy dinners at $200 each:	$10,400
52 dinners at the local place at $100 each:	$5,200
lease upgrade on two Mercedes:	$14,400
overboard holiday party for 50 friends:	$7,500
extravagant Christmas gifts:	$3,000
golf club membership for two:	$5,000
"Spoil 'em" presents for eight grandchildren:	$4,000
52 spa treatments:	$5,200

10 percent charity/church tithing:	$9,500
"Where did that money go?" money:	$8,800
Total:	$95,000

(Again, some of these expenditures are arbitrary. You might not, for example, enjoy traveling abroad. Or you might find your grandchildren deplorable. In reviewing this list, make whatever substitutions you like, so long as they are in the same expense categories.)

Overall, this is a very luxurious lifestyle, wouldn't you say? Not only would you be living in a house that's nice (in California/New York/Florida) or even great (in the rest of the country), driving luxury cars, playing golf, eating out, and taking enviable vacations, you'd also be sharing your good fortune with loved ones and giving to charity.

Again, this budget is based on the presumption that you are a two-person family.

The most important adjustment you'll have to make if you want to get rich while the kids are still home is that some significant percentage of your luxury spending would have to go toward education. Whether that's $5,000 a year or $30,000 depends on how much you value private schools.

Otherwise, the modifications would be pretty easy: you would still take vacations, but they might be to theme parks and camping grounds. You would still eat out several times a week, but there would be less sushi and more hamburger. You would still be able to drive a luxury car, but it might be built on a truck frame.

THE NEXT LEVEL: LIVING ON A $5.5 MILLION NEST EGG

If you had a net worth of $5 million or $6 million, what would your lifestyle look like?

A $5.5 million net worth returning 10 percent is $550,000 a year, or $357,500 after paying 35 percent in taxes. Deduct $90,000 for your housing expenses, another $30,000 for upkeep and utilities, $27,500 for food, clothing, and miscellaneous . . . and you'd end up with $210,000 a year to spend on discretionary items.

Let's see how $210,000 pans out:

10-day Hawaiian vacation for two:	$10,000
10-day London vacation for two:	$10,000
10-day Istanbul trip for two:	$15,000
2 four-day weekends in New York City:	$12,000
52 very fancy meals at $500 each:	$26,000
52 semi-fancy meals at $200 each:	$10,400
104 meals at the local place at $100 each:	$10,400
lease upgrade on two Mercedes:	$14,400
overboard holiday party for 100 friends:	$14,000
extravagant Christmas gifts:	$5,400
golf club membership for two:	$5,000
"Spoil 'em" presents for eight grandchildren:	$4,000
100 spa treatments:	$10,000
10 percent charity/church tithing:	$21,000
"Where did that money go?" money:	$15,000
2 season tickets for an NBA team:	$8,000
tennis club membership/lessons for two:	$5,000
slightly used Ski-Doo snowmobile:	$3,000
120 sessions with a personal trainer:	$11,400
Total:	$210,000

Living like this takes a lot of effort. Spending this much money requires diligence, determination, and imagination. For one thing, you must be willing to eat out four nights a week. You must devote nearly all your spare time to golfing, tennis, spa treatments, and professional basketball games. You would have to eschew low-cost leisure activities like reading, hiking, and fishing (except for deep-sea fishing in luxury spots), and you'd have to . . .

Okay, I'm kidding—or at least half-kidding—to make a point. You don't need $5 million or $6 million in the bank to enjoy a very good lifestyle.

But since this book is called *Seven Years to Seven Figures*, let's push on and describe the sort of lifestyle you'd have to maintain to be able to spend the income generated from a nest egg of $9 million.

THE ULTIMATE LIFESTYLE

Again, $9 million at 10 percent will yield an income of $900,000. After paying 35 percent of that to Uncle Sam, you'd have $585,000 to spend on yourself and your spouse.

If you spent 25 percent of that (or $146,250 a year) on housing, you'd be living in luxury even in California, Florida, or Manhattan.

Figure $45,000 a year for upkeep and utilities, a whopping $50,000 a year for food and clothing (let's stick to Italian designers, please), and you're left with about $345,000 a year.

How could you get rid of $345,000 a year?

10-day Hawaiian vacation for two:	$10,000
10-day London vacation for two:	$10,000
10-day Istanbul trip for two:	$15,000
4 four-day weekends in New York City:	$24,000
52 very fancy meals at $500 each:	$26,000
52 semi-fancy meals at $200 each:	$10,400
104 meals at the local place at $100 each:	$10,400
lease upgrade on two Mercedes:	$14,400
way overboard holiday party for 100 friends:	$20,000
ultra-extravagant Christmas gifts:	$10,000
golf club membership for two:	$5,000
"*Really* spoil 'em" presents for eight grandchildren:	$8,000
104 spa treatments:	$10,400
charity/church tithing:	$40,000
"Where did that money go?" money:	$24,000
2 season tickets for an NBA team:	$8,000
tennis club/membership for two:	$5,000
120 sessions with a personal trainer:	$11,400
Bose Home Theater System:	$4,100
Sony VAIO notebook computers for you, your spouse, and all eight grandchildren:	$22,000
high-definition mini-camcorder:	$3,600
Matching diamond and platinum ring, earrings, and pendant from Tiffany:	$16,250
52 weeks of fresh flower delivery:	$4,450

3 widescreen plasma TV sets:	$15,000
stereo systems for two cars:	$4,000
digital cameras for you, your spouse, and all eight grandchildren:	$13,600
Total:	$345,000

As you can see, you can live reasonably well—without working—on a net worth of a million dollars. Having $2 million or $3 million in the bank makes life easy. If you target the $5 million to $9 million range, you'll be able to enjoy all the luxuries you have ever imagined . . . and still have money left over that you won't know what to do with. (Of course, if you decide to target the higher end of the seven-figure range, you'll have to expect to work harder and take more risk to achieve your goal.)

Well? Have you picked the level of wealth that you want to attain? Good.

Now take that number (any seven-figure number between $1 million and $9 million) and subtract your current net worth (not counting the value of your house) from it. If, for example, you currently have a $500,000 net worth and have decided to go for a $3 million net worth lifestyle, your actual wealth-building objective should be $2.5 million.

If your net worth is negative (with liabilities outweighing your assets), your ultimate target will increase by that number. For example, if your net worth is a negative half-million now and your lifestyle preference is in the $4 million range, your wealth-building target should be $4.5 million.

The next step is to take this target number and divide it by one of the divisors listed in Table 2.1. The number you choose will depend on either (a) the amount of interest your investments will earn or (b) the amount of money you will be able to invest.

Don't be intimidated by the numbers. We'll walk through them together.

First, let's focus on Table 2.1. The divisors in this table are based on the amount of interest your investments will earn.

An average ROI of 10 percent a year is very reasonable, so let's start there.

Table 2.1: Divisors for Different ROIs Over 7 Years

Percent ROI	Divisor
10	10.44
15	12.73
20	15.50
25	18.84
30	22.86
35	27.66
40	33.39
45	40.20

Let's say your target net worth is $3.5 million. You have an investment portfolio that will generate annual returns of 10 percent . . . and you don't want to wait a minute longer than seven years to reach your target.

Take a look at Table 2.1. To the right of 10 percent—the amount of interest your investments will earn—is the number 10.44.

Divide your target ($3.5 million) by 10.44.

After plugging these two figures into your calculator, you'll end up with $335,250. This means you will have to invest $335,250 each year to reach your target. Remember, this isn't a one-time investment of $335,000. You need to be diligent about stowing away that money every year for seven years. And your investment must be generating an average return of 10 percent. If you can do that, you'll easily reach your goal.

The purpose of this exercise is not to suggest that you need to boost your income to $335,000 this year, but to demonstrate an important point: reaching a seven-figure net worth in seven years or less *can't be done without a really big income.*

Investing over $300,000 a year is not easy, but—all other things being equal—it's what you would need to do to achieve $3.5 million in seven years.

BUT WHAT IF YOU CAN'T POSSIBLY SAVE $335,000 A YEAR?

You can achieve the same level of wealth with a smaller investment *if* you can get a better ROI than 10 percent. What if you could get an

ROI of 20 percent? How much of a yearly investment would you need to make then?

Looking again at Table 2.1, you can see that your divisor for a 20 percent ROI is 15.5. Divide $3.5 million by 15.5 and you end up with the yearly investment of $225,800.

And what if you could get a 30 percent ROI?

That's $3.5 million divided by 22.86, which is a yearly investment of $153,100.

And you'd do even better if you could earn a higher return—say, 50 percent each year.

If you could invest $100,000 a year and earn a 50 percent return, on the average, over seven years, your money would mount up as follows:

Initial Investment: $100,000
Year One: $150,000
Year Two: $375,000
Year Three: $712,000
Year Four: $1,218,750
Year Five: $1,978,125
Year Six: $3,117,187
Year Seven: $4,825,780

That's pretty impressive, don't you agree? And you should see how the numbers add up if you keep going till Year Ten.

How do you know what amount of interest you need on your investments in order to reach your target in seven years?

There are two ways to do this. You can either go back to Table 2.1 and try out different divisors until you get a yearly investment figure that looks reasonable. Or you can look at Table 2.2, where I've done some of the work for you.

This table illustrates the fundamental arguments I'm making in this book:

- You can't get wealthy quickly unless you can afford to invest a lot of money.
- To invest a lot of money, you need to make a lot of money.

Table 2.2: Seven-Year Annual Investment Necessary With Different Rates of Interest

Target Net Worth	1 million	2 million	3 million	3.5 million	5 million	7 million	9 million
10% ROI	$95,823	$191,646	$287,470	$335,381	$479,116	$670,762	$862,409
15% ROI	$78,574	$157,148	$235,723	$275,010	$392,871	$550,020	$707,168
20% ROI	$64,520	$129,040	$193,560	$225,820	$322,600	$451,640	$580,679
25% ROI	$53,073	$106,147	$159,220	$185,757	$265,367	$371,513	$477,660
30% ROI	$43,749	$87,498	$131,247	$153,121	$218,745	$306,243	$393,741
35% ROI	$36,148	$72,296	$108,444	$126,518	$180,740	$253,036	$325,332
40% ROI	$29,945	$59,890	$89,835	$104,807	$149,724	$209,614	$269,504
45% ROI	$24,874	$49,749	$74,623	$87,060	$124,372	$174,121	$223,870
50% ROI	$20,722	$41,444	$62,166	$72,527	$103,610	$145,054	$186,498

- If you can get above-average (i.e., above 10 percent) returns on your money, you don't have to save as much money each year.
- And even if you could get an average annual rate of return of 45 percent (which is very difficult), you'd still have to be able to invest a lot of money every year.

The *Seven Years to Seven Figures* wealth-building program is based on experience. My experience (and the experiences of the successful men and women you'll read about later in this book) tells me that you can't get rich that fast unless you dramatically increase your income.

There are many ways to dramatically increase your income, and none of them involves scrimping and saving pennies. As you'll soon see, you can start making enough dough to put away between $20,000 and $200,000 every year by doing two things:

- Investing directly in a brand-new business
- Investing directly in real estate

There are all sorts of ways to improve the *rate of return* you are currently getting on your stocks and bonds. But this book is devoted to telling you how some of the people I know—mentors, protégés, and colleagues—have achieved seven-figure wealth in seven years or less by doing those two things: investing in new businesses and real estate.

HOW MUCH OF YOUR INCOME SHOULD YOU BE SAVING?

You want to save as much as you can without that miserable penny-pinching feeling. Said differently, you want to save as much as you can while you are still "living rich."

For most people, "living rich" means spending more than they make. Indeed, studies show that the more people make, the more they spend.

All those mortgages, credit cards, car loans, and other personal debts really add up. In fact, according to *USA Today*, the average American household had personal debt in the range of $84,454 in 2003.

Smart savers (i.e., wealth builders) understand that they don't have to spend a whole lot to live well. They know that the best things in life really are free—requiring nothing more than an investment of time and love. And that the next-best things—the material things that make life good—can be purchased wisely and enjoyed forever.

Smart savers know that you don't have to crank up the spending as your income increases. On the contrary, the percentage of their income that is saved increases as their income increases.

Many financial planners recommend a savings rate of 10 percent of your net (after-tax) income. My recommendation is 15 percent of your gross (pre-tax) income. That's an aggressive savings plan—but if you incorporate my ideas for living rich into your budgeting, it can be done.

The average college graduate makes about $35,000 these days. Fifteen percent of that is $5,250. At the other end of the age spectrum, the average baby boomer makes $57,700. Fifteen percent of that is $8,655. Either way, that's a lot of money to sock away every year.

If you have your own business (either a full-time business or something that you do on weekends) and invest in real estate, you will be able to realize significant tax savings, even at the $35,000 income level. As a ballpark figure, I believe you should be able to reduce your taxes—state, local, and federal—to no more than $5,000 a year. That would leave you with $30,000 to live on.

Smart savers with that kind of modest income would leverage up their lifestyles by sharing living quarters with one or more people. Having your own room in a three- or four-bedroom house is generally cheaper than having a one-bedroom house or apartment of your own. A $10,000 allocation toward the rent/mortgage and utilities would leave you about $15,000 a year (or $1,250 a month) to spend on food, clothing, and fun. By shopping wisely (vintage stores instead of The Gap; natural foods instead of manufactured crap; homemade meals instead of restaurant dates), you could live very well—even richly—on $1,250 a month.

In *Automatic Wealth*, I suggested many ways to boost your income to $150,000 in three years or less. In *Seven Years to Seven Figures*, I am providing specific examples of people who have done that . . . and better.

With an income of $150,000 a year, you can expect to be paying about 25 percent of that—or $37,500—in taxes. The rest ($112,500) would be available for housing, "living rich," and savings.

Assuming you paid $36,000 for housing and associated costs, and then tripled your living-rich expenses to $30,000 a year ($2,500 a month), you'd have $46,000 for savings. That represents a savings rate of 40 percent. Split your housing costs with a roommate, and you'll be able to save 55 percent of your income!

Saving half of your gross income may seem insane, but it's entirely possible. And it can be done without pinching pennies. I have never denied myself anything I wanted. I have, however, learned how to make thoughtful buying decisions. By investing in products and services that add true value to my life, that enrich my life in meaningful ways, I've been able to save at least 50 percent of my gross income for the past 20 years—even now that I'm paying as much as 35 percent of my gross income in taxes.

If you would like to maximize your wealth-building progress (i.e., accelerate the pace at which you acquire wealth), I recommend that you set for yourself the following rate-of-income saving targets:

If you are making less than $30,000 a year:	15%
More than $30,000 but less than $50,000:	20%
More than $50,000 but less than $150,000:	25%
More than $150,000 but less than $300,000:	30%
More than $300,000 but less than $500,000:	35%
More than $1 million but less than $2 million:	40%
More than $2 million but less than $5 million:	50%
More than $5 million:	55%

In the introduction to this book, I said that getting wealthy has three components:

1. How long you invest
2. How much you invest
3. What rate of return you get on your investments

With our *Seven Years to Seven Figures* time limit, you have to commit yourself to both investing more every year and getting a higher ROI.

As you work your way through this book, I'll teach you how to do it. I'll tell you exactly how to approach different types of investments . . . from real estate to stocks to your very own business.

I'll also teach you about valuable income-accelerating techniques that will make it possible for you to invest a bigger chunk every year.

For now, just get some numbers in your head.

If you have a lot of money to invest right now, think in terms of 20 percent, 15 percent, or even 10 percent returns. (This means you'll be able to do most of your investing in the stock market.)

If you don't have a lot to invest, your ROI numbers will need to be higher. To get 25 percent to 35 percent, you can expect to be investing in a mixture of real estate and stocks. To get 40 percent, 45 percent, or 50 percent, you'll need to invest in real estate, stocks, and small businesses. And if your situation requires you to be generating extremely high returns—50 percent or more—to reach your wealth goal . . . the only way you'll be able to do it is by starting your own business.

The people I profiled for this book have all invested in real estate or stocks. But they have all made huge amounts of money through the various businesses they've started or helped run.

With a combination of stocks, real estate, and business savvy, you can follow in their footsteps.

And just think. You are now on your way to achieving a seven-figure net worth within the next seven years!

PART II

EIGHT STORIES, EIGHT SUCCESSES

When I first thought of the *Seven Years to Seven Figures* concept, I got lots of positive feedback. A marketing group I met with liked the idea, and my publisher and the people in their marketing department thought it would sell.

Buoyed by their enthusiasm, I agreed to write the book. But several weeks later, when I told my writing assistant about our next exciting assignment, she sent me a simple e-mail.

"Sounds great. One question: Can it really be done?"

An embarrassing moment.

I realized that I hadn't asked myself that simple question. I was sure I could come up with a *theory* about how to make a million dollars (or more) in seven years (or fewer).

But that wasn't the question my assistant was asking. In her bright-eyed, post-Princeton, trusting-yet-skeptical innocence, she really wanted to know if it was possible to become that rich that fast.

I thought about it. And then I thought about it some more. And I realized that the answer was a resounding *yes*!

I had made my first million in fewer than seven years. So, too, had some of my wealthy friends. More important, after I came back into the business world at the end of my first retirement in 1989, I worked with a dozen or so smart, ambitious people (some younger and some middle-aged) who had done very well for themselves. A number of them had even become multimillionaires. I wondered, "How many years, exactly, did it take them to get rich? And how did they do it?"

That's what Part II of this book is all about: the actual habits, patterns, and practices of eight people I know who became wealthy very quickly.

Pay close attention–and you could be on your way to more wealth than you ever imagined.

CHAPTER 3

AUDREY MAXWELL*

How a Good Employee Can Become
a Great Partner, Build a Dream House,
and Become a Millionaire in Seven Years

When I approached Audrey Maxwell about being a subject for this book, she told me I had the wrong girl.

"I'm not a millionaire," she said. "In fact, I'm nowhere near it."

But because she was a partner in a business I'm familiar with, I had a different take on her net worth. "Just for the heck of it," she agreed to do a quick calculation of her assets. This is what we discovered.

Her house, net of her mortgage, was worth $550,000.

She had $40,000 in bonds.

Her stock portfolio was worth about $20,000.

She had $135,000 in her retirement plan.

And she had $30,000 in cash.

That came to a grand total of $775,000.

"What did I tell you?" she said.

"But what about your business?" I asked her.

"What about it?"

"You do have equity in it, don't you?"

"Well, of course I do," she said.

"And your equity is worth something."

"Well I guess it is, but I'm not planning to sell my shares."

"You don't have to sell your shares to recognize their value," I reminded her.

Normally, valuing shares in a small, privately held business can be dicey. But in Audrey's case, the matter had been settled. Soon after the business began making profits, the partners got together and established a way to value the business. They agreed, and incorporated into their partnership agreement, that the company would be worth the sum of three years' net earnings divided by three times four. And they agreed that if a partner wanted to cash out, he could sell his shares to the other partners based on that formula.

This is a relatively simple yet common way to evaluate the kind of business Audrey is running. It is based on profits. It says, essentially, that the company is worth four times the profits of an average year.

In the past three years, Audrey's company has made a total of $2.2 million in profits ($500,000, $700,000, and $1,000,000). That averages out to $733,000 per year. Multiply $733,000 by four and you get a valuation of $2,933,000 for 100 percent of the stock. That makes Audrey's 12.5 percent share worth $366,000.

Add $366,000 to the $775,000 she thought she was worth and you have a total net worth of more than $1.1 million.

"Congratulations," I told her. "You're a millionaire."

Being a millionaire is no great shakes today, but it's a heck of a lot better than being broke. And that's what Audrey was seven years ago. Not just broke, but worse than broke.

A MILLION-DOLLAR CAREER

Audrey is an interesting illustration of what often happens to people who are happy to go with the flow and don't pay too much attention to their financial well-being. It is both a study of how to make a good income vanish into thin air and an example of how quickly you can go from broke to wealthy if you apply your knowledge and experience to a pragmatic, wealth-building game plan.

Audrey's business career began just after she graduated from college in 1983. Armed with a BA in advertising, she took a job in the data input department of a small publishing company that sold its products through direct mail.

Over the next 10 years, she worked in practically every area of that business—from fulfillment to production to editorial and, finally, marketing.

"I understood the mechanics of running a publishing company. And I got a good understanding of how direct marketing works," she said.

The company Audrey worked for was enjoying strong growth. During the time she was there, sales virtually exploded—from $1 million to over $100 million by 1993. Then it was broken up into several direct-marketing companies and sold—and Audrey was given the opportunity to be vice president of one of those companies.

"Because I knew more about running a direct-marketing business than my boss did at the time," Audrey explained, "I was given, as an incentive, a stake in the company's increasing value. The deal was that I would get a certain percentage of the profits every year above a certain base line, plus that same percentage if and when the company was ever sold."

It was indeed sold about two years later, and Audrey's bonus was more than $100,000. "That was a huge amount of money to me," she admitted. "But I burned through it pretty quickly—going on a six-week trip to Europe, buying a car . . . you name it.

"I had a really great year. There's no doubt about that," she said. "But it would have been smarter to put some of that money into a savings account."

After her spending spree was over, Audrey went back to work as an employee for another direct-marketing company. "It was a great company that I was happy to be a part of," she said. "But it was tough going from running my own show to being an employee again."

But Audrey persisted, and her experience and dedication paid off again. From a middle-management position with a starting salary of $40,000, she moved steadily up through the ranks.

By 1999, Audrey was making $50,000 and living well. "I had a two-bedroom apartment with a balcony across the street from the beach, a job I liked, and an active social life with friends and family."

Audrey was enjoying a lifestyle that most people hope to attain when they are retired. "The only problem," she said, "is that I was spending my income as fast as I was making it.

"One day, inspired by a magazine article, I decided to calculate my net worth. I had about $5,000 in a stock-funded IRA and $500 in cash. Both my apartment and my car were rented—so no equity there. And I had slowly racked up about $12,000 worth of credit card debt.

"According to the magazine article, my financial shape was 'worse than average' for my age and income. That shocked me, since I viewed myself as both financially conservative and relatively successful."

Audrey had good reason to be surprised. After all, she had been earning an above-average salary for most of her career. But she was a single woman supporting herself on a single income, and she had never developed the habit of saving money.

In the 16 years she'd been working, Audrey had earned more than $800,000. Yet she had managed to save only $5,000—less than 1 percent of that income.

"It was embarrassing to realize that I had saved so little money, frustrating to think that I probably should have had at least 10 times that much by then," Audrey said. "But it was also scary to think that if I ever got sick or lost my job, I'd have nothing to fall back on.

"And, as I found out, I wasn't the only one with that problem," Audrey said. "At an informal business lunch one day, two of my colleagues, both freelance copywriters, admitted that they had been doing the same thing. They were making more than I was, but they were spending their money just as fast."

All three agreed that it was impossible to save money, no matter how much you make. "That made me feel better for a while," Audrey said, "but when I repeated the conversation to my father, he laughed and set me straight. 'That's what I used to tell myself when I was your age,' he said. 'But when your older brother was born, I stopped making excuses and began saving.'

"My father made me realize that I was too old to be living on a spend-it-as-you-make-it basis. He was right. As a single woman, I knew I had to be prepared to take care of myself—both now and in the future. So although friends and family have always come first for me, I had to make saving money a major priority."

As it turned out, Audrey's two copywriting friends had had a similar revelation. "They confessed their financial predicament to a very successful man who had always acted as a mentor to them," Audrey remembered, "and he told them pretty much the same thing my father told me. He told them to start some sort of side business that would add to their income as freelance copywriters—money that they could start saving.

"So that's what they decided to do. And the business idea they came up with was to market a home-study program to teach others what they knew how to do best: write advertising copy."

Audrey's two friends had roughed out the idea for the business—what the program would consist of and how they would sell it through direct mail. And their mentor even volunteered to come up with the necessary start-up funds and act as their business consultant in exchange for a percentage of their new venture. But they needed someone to run the business on a day-to-day basis.

"Since my two friends were already making six figures writing copy," Audrey said, "they weren't inclined to give up their day jobs. And since they knew that I had lots of experience in all aspects of the direct-marketing business, they proposed that they would write the product and the promotions and I would run the business."

Within 60 days, they were in business. "At first, I kept my day job, too," Audrey said. "I didn't want to quit it until I was sure our business was going to succeed."

Although they started their business on a shoestring budget, Audrey was able to take advantage of her contacts in the direct-marketing industry and secure advertising slots in publications on a "pay us later" or "pay us half of what you make" basis. "It was a combination of being sweet and begging," Audrey said.

They patched together an ad that they tested in five different investment newsletters. "Three of those five media were completely unsuccessful," Audrey said. "But one of them was good and one of them was great."

In the direct-marketing business, you can create a profitable business even if four-fifths of your initial marketing efforts fail. What you do is identify a large group of potential customers who should respond well to your offer. You do a test mailing to a small portion of the names on that "list." If it's successful, you "roll out" by sending your promotion to more names on the list. And you use the money you make from those mailings to find additional lists that will work for you.

That's what Audrey and her three partners did. After they found one list that responded well to their offer, they found another list that worked. And then, several months later, they wrote a second direct-mail package—one that scored a home run.

"After a few months of trepidation, we were solidly in business," Audrey said. "It was a very exciting time."

At that point, leaving her comfortable, $50,000 a year job wasn't a hard choice for Audrey, even though it meant a big drop in salary—to $36,000 a year—since the new company needed every dollar it could get to spend on marketing.

"I was willing to go backward in my income for a few years," Audrey said, "because, as a partner, I knew that if I worked hard and the company was successful, I'd have a piece of the action. Meanwhile, I was forcing myself to save at least a little money every month."

As the company grew, so did Audrey's compensation. Within three years, she had even surpassed her previous salary. She was saving money, but her retirement account was growing slowly.

"I realized that unless something changed I was going to have to keep working for pretty much the rest of my life," she said.

"I talked to a number of people about my situation—including my dad—and they all said the same thing: I had to find some way to make our little business more profitable."

The business had been growing at a steady pace, but most of the profits were being reinvested into marketing and there wasn't much left over at the end of the year to distribute to Audrey and her partners.

"It was about that time that I began reading Michael Masterson's e-zine *Early to Rise*. I liked the fact that it offered a variety of motivating, educational, and practical advice every day. I paid most attention to the advice about business building and marketing.".

One of the *ETR* articles that strongly influenced Audrey was about how you can make a product line much more lucrative by testing different direct-mail offers.

"The article said that it's wrong to assume that the price you've been charging for years is the best one," Audrey said. "Sometimes you can achieve a breakthrough just by tinkering with the terms or refund."

That's what Audrey did. The home-study program they'd been selling was priced at $500, and there was only one payment option:

cash up front. Audrey tested a number of different offers, including one with a $39 down payment and automatically billed monthly follow-up payments of $39 each.

"This turned out to be a major boost for our business," Audrey said. "Not only did we more than quintuple our response rate, the average lifetime value of each customer we acquired nearly doubled."

Sales lifted immediately—and by the end of that first year, profits had doubled.

WHEN YOUR SUPPORT NET DISAPPEARS

"I was feeling pretty good," Audrey said. "But then my father—who had been helping me a lot since the business began—passed away."

Suddenly, a powerful force in Audrey's life was missing.

"I was moving in the right direction," Audrey said. "But all of a sudden I felt out there on my own."

Having recently purchased a house, Audrey had a mortgage, property taxes, and insurance bills to pay, not to mention the old balances that she was still paying off on her credit cards. She knew that she was at a crossroads. She could retreat to her make-it-and-spend-it days— and it was tempting. Or she could "grow up quickly" and accelerate everything she had been doing to become financially independent.

"For the first time in my life, I had no one to count on but myself."

Audrey decided to take charge of her financial future. She increased the percentage of her income that she had started putting into bonds and low-risk mutual funds. And she began investing $10,000 a year in a 401(k) account.

"When I first read Michael Masterson's advice in *ETR* to save 15 percent of your salary, I thought, 'He's crazy.' But when I put that advice into practice, it was easy. I had the money automatically deducted from my bank account every month and transferred to my savings. So long as it was 'gone' before I could touch it, saving 10 percent and then 20 percent was no problem."

At the same time as she was increasing her savings, Audrey redoubled her efforts to make the business grow. "Saving a bigger percentage of my paycheck was helping, but it wasn't going to get me rich fast. To make a dramatic change in my financial situation, I knew I had to make a bigger income—and I realized that the way to do that would be to increase our company's profits.

"We were making a couple hundred thousand dollars a year at that time. It was better than losing money, but nobody was getting very excited about it. I figured if I could get that number up to, say, half a million in profits, I could expect to see a percentage of that by way of salary increases and bonuses. And if I could eventually get our profits beyond the million-dollar mark, I'd be in a position to demand a considerably higher compensation package."

Changing the offer from a $500 cash-up-front deal to automatic billing at $39 per month was a major step in the right direction. But another trick she learned from *ETR*—"ratcheting up the back end"—led to another leap forward in terms of profits.

By producing a line of high-quality ancillary products—and selling them to existing customers at high prices—Audrey's company dramatically increased profits.

Now that the company was making more than a million dollars a year in profits, Audrey could easily justify her salary of more than $100,000. Plus, she was receiving a bonus every year . . . and her share of profit distributions.

"Last year, I made almost six times what I was making before we started this company," she said. "I'm glad I had the guts to quit my previous job. It would have been easy to stay on that career path, because I liked the work and I was getting steady raises. But if I had, I'd never be where I am today—either in terms of money or job satisfaction."

Their company works, Audrey says, because it is based on applying solid direct-marketing principles to quality products. She believes in the products she sells, and says that one of the best things about her job is that she gets to hear how they've helped so many people. Audrey has received hundreds of letters from customers who have used her company's home-study products to earn extra income and enjoy better lives.

Since implementing those two fundamental marketing strategies—changing the offer and beefing up the back end—Audrey's company has become more and more profitable every year. And it's grown internally, too, blossoming from the four initial partners to more than 20 employees.

Those employees are another reason Audrey's company is so profitable.

"They range in age from 23 to 82. And they really care about what they're doing," Audrey said. "They are all energetic . . . creative . . . and dedicated."

With strong skills, a team of intelligent, motivated employees, and a solid savings plan, Audrey has achieved financial independence. She has built a successful business that will fund an early retirement.

And the best part? Her success can be yours.

FOLLOW AUDREY'S PATH TO SEVEN FIGURES

Audrey's seven-year path from Nowheresville to Happytown was the result of three smart moves:

- She converted her reputation as a good worker into sweat equity in a business.
- She discovered a way to dramatically increase her company's customer base by reinventing the price of her main product.
- She bought a home in a good neighborhood at a good price.

Converting Your Reputation into Sweat Equity

When Audrey's copywriting friends asked her to take part in their business, she expected it to be a job pretty much like the jobs she'd done in the past. She figured she'd be paid a decent salary, with fair-to-good increases each year and some fringe benefits.

But a funny thing happened halfway through the first meeting with her future partners. She realized just how invaluable she could be in helping them make their idea a success.

Audrey knew from the get-go that she and her copywriting buddies brought different strengths to the table. Audrey's strength was on the business and marketing side of the company, while they were experts on the communication and product development side. They had zero interest in running the day-to-day operations of the business—which meant that, without Audrey, they'd either have to take over an area of business that they didn't enjoy or go through the hassle of finding and breaking in someone new. This put Audrey in an excellent position. She knew that she could do—and do well—the marketing, customer service, management, and product fulfillment tasks that her partners loathed.

By the end of the meeting, Audrey was excited about the opportunity. "I wanted in. And I knew they wanted me for the job. But, I wanted to be more than just an employee.

"I've never been very aggressive professionally . . . never asked for raises or made big demands. Now, all of a sudden, I knew that I was going to ask for equity in this business.

"I bought some time. Asked the guys if I could get back to them in the morning with some ideas about how we could proceed."

As soon as Audrey left the meeting, she started to devise a plan. She figured that they would come into the meeting armed with reasons why they couldn't/wouldn't want to give her a piece of their pie. So she decided to beat them to the punch and walk in with a sheet of paper with the heading: Seven Reasons You Should Give Audrey a Share of This Business.

Audrey used one of the principles of direct marketing to compose her list: she focused on her prospects, not on herself. Rather than explaining what being a partner would mean for *her*, she listed all the benefits it would have for *her partners*. They wouldn't have to interact with customers. They wouldn't have to plan the marketing campaigns. They wouldn't need to deal with pricing or any of the day-to-day issues that come up in any business. She would prove to them that she was valuable, that she was going to make their lives easier, and that she was going to help the business succeed.

"Frankly, I was scared," Audrey said. "They looked over my list and asked me to step out of the room for five minutes . . . and when I came back in, they told me that they agreed with everything on my list, and were going to give me a big chunk of equity in the business.

"That's how effective that little sheet of paper was!"

HOW TO GET YOUR BOSS TO GIVE YOU EQUITY IN THE BUSINESS

A good deal of Audrey's financial windfall came from the stake she had in the company she was running. By switching from a relatively safe position as a middle manager with a larger company to the top position in a fledgling business, she exchanged safety for the chance to earn more money in three ways:

- Her salary could increase dramatically.
- She would get yearly bonuses as the company grew.
- As a partner/shareholder, she was entitled to a percentage of profit distributions.

Getting equity in a business without investing in it isn't easy. But if you can work your way up to the position of CEO, you will have a good chance to get, at the very least, an incentive-based plan that equates with equity.

Getting wealthy as an employee involves four steps:

1. Get a marketing, sales, or other key job with a company that has growth potential.
2. Make yourself invaluable to that company by helping it grow.
3. Make yourself known as a dependable, trustworthy money-maker.
4. Convince the stockholders that the company will be more profitable if they give you profit-based incentives.

Step 1: Getting the Right Job with a Good Company

In assessing the job you're going to do, give serious consideration to the person you'll be reporting to, the part of the business you'll be working in, and the business itself.

- What you want in a boss is a smart, experienced person who is going places.
- What you want in a department or division is an orientation toward sales.
- What you want in a company is the potential for significant growth.
- And what you want in the industry, too, is growth potential.

You should opt for a smaller, faster-growing company over a larger, staid business. The larger business will give you more perks and the appearance of more stability, but the smaller, faster-growing company will give you a much greater chance to boost your income.

If you are not already committed to working in a particular type of business, I'd recommend one that gives you complete control over the entire selling process, from inventing the product to closing the sale and even going back to the customer for more sales.

In the age of the Internet and globalization, having control over the entire selling process is invaluable. To create your product, you can use anyone the world over. And you can sell to the entire world, too.

So if you can't figure out what you want to do, but want to get wealthy while you figure it out, consider getting into a business like manufacturing.

Step 2: Making Yourself Invaluable to Your Company

If you want to increase your income, your first objective should be to transform yourself into a more valuable employee. You can do that by:

- Working longer hours

There is no better way to demonstrate your commitment to your company than by getting to work earlier than everybody else and staying later.

- Understanding your responsibilities

You may have received a job description when you were hired and it may do a pretty good job of telling you what you have to do. But until you figure out how the company works, how it makes its money, how it creates a profit, and what place it occupies in the marketplace, you won't understand what really matters.

- Working harder

You want a higher income. You recognize that you can expect to get one only by becoming a more valuable employee. Working longer hours and understanding how your job affects the company's bottom line are critical components . . . but it is old-fashioned hard work that sets you apart.

- Working smarter

Ask questions. Read memos. Take work-related courses. Do everything you can to make yourself smarter and more effective at what you do.

- Helping your boss do better

Doing your own job well is good. But doing that *and* helping your boss do his job well is a whole lot better. In most businesses, most of the time, power is transferred from the boss to his best employee. If that's the way your business works, when you help your boss move up by making him look good, he'll do the same for you.

Keep in mind that, as an employee, you have a distinct advantage over your boss, because you are probably, in some way or another, closer to the action. You may be closer to the customers or to the production process or to the fulfillment problems. You may be closer to what goes on internally—the strife and turmoil among employees. Whatever it is, you have an opportunity to help your boss succeed by coming up with perspectives, questions, and solutions he can't clearly see.

Do that and he'll be your strongest supporter when it comes time to upgrade your income.

TRANSITIONING FROM "VALUABLE" TO "INVALUABLE"

If getting better-than-average pay increases can be achieved by learning to become a better-than-average worker, how do you get spectacular pay raises?

You guessed it. Good employees earn good salaries because they are valued. But great employees earn amazing salaries because they are considered *invaluable*.

Let's take a moment to define terms here, because words like "valuable" and "invaluable" are often too liberally used. A boss may say that her personal assistant is invaluable when she simply means that the assistant takes care of all her needs and makes her life a lot easier.

But is the assistant invaluable in the sense of being worth an almost unlimited amount of money? Would she double her assistant's salary to keep her? Triple it?

You want to be considered invaluable, but not the kind of invaluable that gets you a pat on the head and an extra $20 a week. To be truly invaluable, you have to be, more or less, irreplaceable. How can you do that?

Well, the truth is you can't do it absolutely. Everybody, including Donald Trump and Oprah Winfrey, is replaceable. But the closer you can get to *seeming to be* irreplaceable, the better your chances of radically increasing your income.

Step 3: Making Yourself Known as a Dependable, Trustworthy Moneymaker

It's not enough to be invaluable. People have to know that you are.

The people who are in charge of the company you work for need to know how good you are. And good means good at making money. No other business skill—not management, not accounting, not production or cost controls or customer service—matters more than the ability to generate sales and profits. If you think otherwise, you are kidding yourself.

As you develop your profit-generating skills, be sure to publicize your progress. Don't toot your own horn too obviously. Disguise your self-promotion efforts as genuine attempts to communicate with your superiors.

One of the best ways to do this is to send out a periodic report on your department's efforts, but designed specifically to highlight the profit-generating accomplishments that you've had a hand in. Another effective strategy is to develop mentor-protégé relationships with a few key people in your company and to chat with them, from time to time, about the challenges and the successes you've experienced.

You have to sell yourself as someone who can bring extra money to the bottom line, because that's what every business, no matter how successful, needs. But you also have to promote yourself as someone who can be trusted. If your boss or mentor thinks you will sell him out to get ahead of him, he will never give you the support you will eventually need to get into a top position.

In summary:

- You have to be seen as trustworthy—someone who won't betray confidences and will repay kindnesses with loyalty.

- You have to be seen as dependable—someone who does what she says she will do, even if it means pulling all-nighters or working over the weekend.
- You have to be seen as a moneymaker—someone who, for example, knows how to run a solid advertising campaign or write great marketing copy or create profitable back-end products.

If you can get the key people in your business to see these three qualities in you, it won't be hard to get yourself into the catbird seat in terms of higher income, profit-based incentives, and even equity in the company.

Step 4: Convincing the Shareholders to Give You
Profit-Based Compensation

Audrey was able to get great raises (from $36,000 to more than $100,000), great bonuses ($40,000 one year), and even equity in the business she worked for, because her partners believed that she could produce a profit.

I can tell you from experience that when you are investing in a new company, there are all sorts of risks at play. Most of those risks involve marketing new products to an unproven market. But one of the most important risks is the chance you take on the CEO. The question is, "Can this person do what is needed to turn a profit?"

When Audrey's copywriting friends invited her to assume a leadership role in the new business they were starting, they did so because they knew she had the qualities necessary for the job. She knew the direct-marketing business backward and forward, had years of experience in management, and had already run a profitable (albeit small) business that had been sold for a profit.

"I had a track record of performance," Audrey said, "which meant that operations was one thing they didn't have to worry about."

When it came time to figure out who was going to get how much equity, the three friends sat down with their fourth partner—the man who was going to come up with the funding as well as be a consultant for the business—and asked him what he thought was fair. He suggested that because he would be raising all of the risk capital, he deserved half of the equity. The other 50 percent should be split between the three working partners, with Audrey's partners each getting close to 19 percent of that equity, and Audrey getting 12.5 percent.

"If we had known how little cash was needed to get the company going or how successful it would eventually become," Audrey said, "we might have tried to raise the money ourselves. Still, getting a percent of the equity without risking any money was a good deal for us. And besides, as working partners, we would also be getting a salary and bonuses."

Because the fledgling company was meant to be grown on a very tight budget, Audrey's initial salary was very low: only $36,000.

"But we all agreed that since I was the only partner working full-time, my salary would be raised to a more reasonable level before we made any profit distributions."

Audrey's willingness to work for less than the $50,000 she had been making was an important symbol of good will and a tangible investment of her faith in the new business. "I think the fact that I was willing to start at a $36,000 salary made a big impression with everybody," Audrey said. "The other partners were contributing some of their spare time to the cause, but nobody but me was taking an actual reduction in salary just to get the business growing."

Audrey's show of faith was repaid as soon as the company had enough money to do it. "We didn't make any profits that first year," Audrey said, "but we came pretty close . . . and the partners were very happy with my efforts."

To indicate their approval, they awarded Audrey a $10,000 cash bonus and told her that they hoped it would be the smallest yearly bonus she would ever receive in the future.

What Audrey did can be done by just about anyone who is interested in getting wealthy without taking the risk of starting his or her own business. The principle behind it—the same direct-marketing principle that Audrey used to come up with the list that convinced her partners to give her a piece of their company—can be applied to all sorts of business situations.

The idea is this: to get your employer to give you a promotion, or an above-average raise, or an incentive-based bonus, or even equity in the business, you need to focus on *his* needs, not yours. That means doing one of two things (or both):

- Find out what his biggest financial problem is, and solve it.
- Discover a new way to increase sales, and put it into action.

When it comes time to demonstrate your value, don't bother with the standard approach of listing your responsibilities, summarizing your track record, and recounting all the projects you've completed.

Those accomplishments may mean a lot to you, but chances are they will mean very little to your boss or your boss's bosses. This conventional approach to self-promotion hardly ever works because it focuses too much on the employee and not enough on the employer.

THE FIRST AND MOST IMPORTANT SECRET TO GETTING WHAT YOU WANT

The most important thing you need to realize about asking for a raise, a bonus, or equity is this: your employer or partner is *not really interested in you*.

He's interested in *himself*. And he's also interested in his business—the problems and the challenges his company faces every day. He may be in need of someone to help him, but he doesn't care about how wonderful that person is. He just wants to know: "Can this person solve my problems?"

If you think of your objective as a direct-marketing problem, it will be relatively easy to achieve.

Direct marketing is the science of creating positive responses with sales letters. By using its proven secrets, you dramatically increase your chances of getting the kind of response you are looking for.

The direct marketer knows that, to make a sale, she can't waste her prospect's time by talking about herself. Everything she writes must be focused on the prospect's problem and how much better life will be after buying the product.

This is exactly what you have to do when you make your case to your boss/partner. You have to let him know that you understand exactly what his problems are and that you have solutions for each and every one of them.

Think of it this way: when seeking a raise/promotion/cut of the business . . .

- Your presentation is like a part of a direct-mail promotion.
- The presentation is intended to sell, so it must be about the prospect's problems, not about your strengths or wishes.
- The prospect—your boss, partner, prospective employer—is the customer.
- You are the product—the product that is going to solve your prospect's problems.

Figure out what your prospect needs in order to make her life better. Does she need someone who can improve her services? Reduce her costs? Increase sales? Reduce the time wasted following up on things? Find out what it is that she needs, and prove that you're the person who can give it to her.

Be specific. Make strong promises.

ANATOMY OF A GREAT SELF-PROMOTION PRESENTATION

A great self-promotion presentation:

- Lets your prospect (your boss/partner/prospective employer) know that you know his goals, problems, objectives, etc.
- Makes the claim that you are the person to solve/achieve them
- Proves that you are that person
- Requests a specific action

Audrey's 12.5 percent stake in the new business didn't seem like it was worth anything in 1999—and it wasn't. But seven years later, in 2006, it's worth more than a third of a million dollars. And if the company continues to grow as it has been, it will be worth more than a million dollars within the next five years.

If you are a good employee now, working for a good company, you should get to work immediately on the four-step plan previously outlined so you can enjoy the increased value of the business you work for within the next seven years.

REINVENTING THE PRICE OF YOUR COMPANY'S PRODUCT TO BOOST GROWTH

In advertising, they say, "Copy is king." By this, they mean that a great sales message is more important than anything else. If you can come up with the right "big idea," as legendary marketer David Ogilvy put it, sales will skyrocket.

Great copy can double response rates and, thus, double sales. But if you want to get beyond that—to increase sales by 300 percent . . . 400 percent . . . even 500 percent—you have to be willing to test your offer.

The offer is what you charge for what you are giving away: the price, guarantee, and payment terms for your product.

Most marketers are content to follow whatever offers are already in place. The usual idea about pricing and guarantees is: "If it ain't broke, why fix it?"

While such thinking is generally sound in business, extreme objectives call for extreme strategies. And that's why, when Audrey realized she had to dramatically increase her company's customer base in order to dramatically increase profits (and her compensation), she decided to take a leap and test a dramatically different pricing structure.

Instead of the lump sum fee of $500 that they'd been charging since the business began, she asked herself, "What would happen if the price were only $100?"

There is a rule in marketing that attempts to answer this question. It's called "elasticity of demand," which means that, in a relatively fixed market, demand for a product will increase by the same percentage as its price decreases. Following this rule, if they dropped their unit price from $500 to $100, they would theoretically sell five times more units.

"It's a great theory," Audrey said, "but this is not a widget we're selling. It's an expensive home-study program. It costs us nearly a hundred dollars to produce, market, and fulfill. Dropping the price to $100 would leave us with little or no profit. So I had to come up with something else."

What Audrey came up with is a strategy known as a "continuity payment" plan, where you drop the immediate price but not the total price. Instead of paying $500 up front, customers had the option of paying a much lower monthly fee. This is the way many people prefer to pay for big-ticket items—cars, homes, furniture. It allows the customer to stretch out the cost over a long period of time.

Offering a continuity payment option made the already attractive home-study program seem even more appealing. Customers who would be turned off by a $500 price tag could pay for the course in small, monthly installments.

Audrey ran three tests. She tested the continuity offer by itself, she tested the single payment offer by itself, and she tested them in combination. The combination was by far the most successful. Now, customers could purchase the course for $500, or they could purchase it for $39 a month.

As soon as Audrey instituted the combined single payment/continuity payment offer, response rates doubled.

Of course, results weren't immediate. In fact, profits lagged a little at first. Because even though the company was attracting twice as many customers, they weren't all paying $500 up front for the program.

But implementing the continuity payment option was a smart long-term decision, and now Audrey's company generates over $200,000 a month in passive income . . . just from the continuity payments. This long-term buildup has allowed her to finance additional promotional activities to ensure that the money keeps rolling in.

The key aspect of Audrey's business was to bring in new customers. But once they ordered the program, she knew that it was also important to develop a line of additional high-quality products that would appeal to the same people.

Sales of those back-end products added significantly to the company's success and growth.

ESTABLISHING THE ALL-IMPORTANT BACK END

The benefit of doubling the company's customer base increased substantially when Audrey added a back-end track to her marketing program. In fact, the lifetime value of her existing customers increased in direct proportion to the number of high-priced back-end products that her company developed to sell to them.

"Your first sale is always your most expensive sale," Audrey explained. "Once you've started a relationship with a customer, each successive sale should be both easier and more lucrative."

This has always been the case, but it is especially true now that the Internet has made communicating with existing customers easy and inexpensive. "Before the Internet, it would cost me at least 50 cents to contact a customer through the mail. Almost $4 if I had to contact them by phone. Now that we have all our customers on the Internet," Audrey explained, "I can 'talk' to them all I want—and that includes conversations about new and upcoming products—for as little as a half a penny per communication."

With familiarity comes trust . . . and with trust comes higher response rates. "The more we talk to our customers, the more likely they are to buy our expensive, back-end products," Audrey explained.

The secret to creating effective back-end products, Audrey said, is to "give your customers more of what they are already getting.

"You don't give them the same exact stuff, because obviously that would be foolish," she said. "But if you can, provide them with a higher level of service or a deluxe version of a product they've already bought."

In Audrey's business, for example, the basic copywriting program (which costs $500) is back-ended by $1,000 to $2,500 specialty seminars . . . bundles of products that sell for between $500 and $1,500 . . . and a super-duper deluxe package of everything they sell for a cool $5,000.

"You'd be amazed at how many people buy that package," Audrey said.

And the reason it sells so well? "Our products are really good. Our customers know us and trust us."

MAKING A WEALTH-WISE DECISION ABOUT YOUR HOME

As I said earlier, Audrey's seven-year path to seven figures was the result of making three smart moves:

- She converted her reputation as a good worker into sweat equity in a business.

- She discovered a way to dramatically increase her company's customer base by reinventing the price of her main product.
- She bought a home in a good neighborhood at a good price.

I've told you about the first two—so now let's look at what happened when she bought her first home.

"I started out renting and got used to it. I had heard that owning was a better move financially, but I didn't have much in the way of savings, so I didn't think much about it.

"But by 1999, I was 38 years old and sick of renting. Even though I didn't think I could afford to buy a house, I really wanted to have a place of my own," Audrey said. "My father told me that I would probably qualify for a low-interest FHA loan, so I decided to give it a shot."

Audrey was hoping to find a house in the town where her business was located, a "friendly beach town with great restaurants and little parks and antique stores." So she concentrated her house-hunting efforts in that community, starting in some of the poorer neighborhoods, because she thought that was all she could afford. "It was discouraging at first," she said, "because I couldn't find anything that I both liked and could handle financially—even with a low-interest loan. But then one day a friend called me and said she'd seen a 'for sale by owner' sign in front of a cute little cottage in an up-and-coming area."

Audrey called the owner at 3:00 in the afternoon and had bought the house by 5:00. She fell in love with the charming cottage and its beautiful garden. And because it was in a "transition" neighborhood, she figured its value was likely to increase.

She bought the house for $135,000. And, having qualified for the FHA loan, she only had to put down three percent—which meant that, including closing costs, she was able to move into her dream house for only $7,000, which she added to the amount of her mortgage loan.

Audrey's home has steadily increased in value. In fact, in the seven years since she bought it, its market value has skyrocketed.

"Owning my own house has been a twofold blessing," Audrey said. "First, because it has given me such an unexpected amount of pleasure. I never realized how much fun it would be to plant a garden, remodel a kitchen, or even make my own mosaic tile stepping stones. Second, because it's increased so much in value.

"It's given me a level of financial security I never had before."

Today, Audrey's house represents a considerable portion of her net worth. There is no doubt that she has been the beneficiary of a major real estate boom in her area. As I write this, property prices are edging down—but Audrey's house will probably hold its value relatively well, since it is in a good neighborhood in a desirable city.

I am not currently advising readers of my e-zine *Early to Rise* (or friends and colleagues, for that matter) to buy real estate. It looks like prices will probably continue to slide for a while.

That said, by the time this book is published, it may once again be the right time to follow Audrey's lead and switch from renting to ownership.

So if you are currently renting, don't feel compelled to rush out and buy something right away. Renting is not always a waste of money. In some times and in some places (like today in the real estate "bubble" markets), it's cheaper and more cost effective to rent and invest the money you save on interest payments, HOA fees, home maintenance, taxes, and insurance. That can easily add up to thousands of dollars a year—cash that will put you in a position to seize the real estate bargains when they come back on the market.

When you buy a home—or any real estate—you can't expect the value of your investment to triple or quadruple in seven years, but you can expect a steady appreciation of about four to six percent a year (based on historical averages). That's assuming you buy reasonably well and hold onto it over the long haul. That four to six percent, by the way, equates to a 20 to 30 percent ROI when you figure in the leverage you get by taking out an 80 percent mortgage.

YOU MAKE YOUR MONEY BY BUYING RIGHT

So, what are some proven strategies for buying real estate?

Most important, make sure you buy at a good price. If you can buy a property significantly below its current market value, you should be able to sit back and watch its value grow.

To find a house that's going for a good price, focus on learning the

ARE YOU BUYING OR SELLING?

Be aware that every business transaction you engage in involves buying and selling. In most cases, a profit is conveyed to the seller. That's why you should look at every business transaction you enter—and I mean "every," from grocery shopping to multimillion-dollar deals—with one question in mind: "Am I buying or selling?" If you are buying, the transaction is probably making you poorer. If you are selling, it is probably making you richer. Even when you buy an investment that you hope will appreciate, the immediate benefit (i.e., profit) goes to the seller—the broker.

In his book *365 Ways to Become a Millionaire* (Plume Books, 1999), Brian Koslow says pretty much the same thing:

"In the United States, it is easier to buy almost anything than it is to sell it. Make sure you count to 10 before buying a house, plane, car, boat, or any other possession that may at some point possess you."

property values of one or two familiar neighborhoods. Properties selling at a discount to market value won't last long, so you'll have to do some legwork to uncover deals and be ready to jump on the bargains the moment they appear.

Look through your local paper and call homes for sale in and around your neighborhood. Find out the address, asking price, and square footage of each one. With that information, you can calculate the average price per square foot of homes in your neighborhood. If, for example, a 1,200 square foot home is on the market for $150,000, the seller is asking $125 per square foot ($150,000/1,200 = $125).

Next, you want to find out the average price per square foot of homes that have actually sold within the last 12 months. Check your local paper or contact your county property appraiser's office. This is public information and very easy to get. (Most counties are online.)

You might find, for example, that the average price per square foot of a home for sale is $125, whereas the average price per square foot of homes that have already sold has been only $100. This kind of information can help you weed the bargains from the bubbles and help you determine if a neighborhood may be on the verge of peaking or just about to take off.

Armed with these numbers, you now have a reliable benchmark to help you quickly determine whether a property represents a good value and a potentially profitable investment.

SNIFFING OUT THE BEST REAL ESTATE DEALS

To get the best property deals on the market, you need to constantly be on the prowl. Justin Ford, editor of *ETR*'s *Main Street Millionaire* real estate program, suggests that you do more than simply read the classifieds or look in real estate magazines.

- Get on good terms with real estate agents. Give them specific criteria for the type of property you want.
- Work the FSBOs (For Sale By Owners)—it worked for Audrey, and it can work for you.
- Keep tabs on foreclosures and government repos.
- Take the long way home by driving through the neighborhood you want to live in on your way to and from work and shopping. When the occasional bargain hits the market, it tends to sell fast. By patrolling your target area, you're much more likely to find out about it before it's snapped up.
- Let all your friends and coworkers know that you're looking for a home, and pass out business cards to people you meet. You'll be surprised at the number of people who will start approaching you about properties they believe look like a good deal . . . just because they know you're in the market.

AUDREY'S FUTURE

When I interviewed Audrey for this book in 2006, she was 45 years old. By most conventional measurements, she was at least 20 years away from retirement.

But Audrey doesn't want to work full-time for another 20 years. "If I could get into a part-time consulting situation by 50 and then retire completely—if I feel like it—at 55, that would be ideal for me," Audrey said.

Could she do that?

Actually, Audrey could retire as early as next year if she is willing to make some major decisions and live on a reasonable budget. Here's how she could do it.

First, she would have to sell her stake in the company for what it should be worth next year, about $450,000. Then, she would have to combine her retirement plan (should be worth $150,000 next year), her stocks (about $30,000 next year), her bonds (about $50,000 next year), and the $30,000 she has in cash into a $710,000 pool that could be invested for the purpose of generating income.

Seven hundred grand invested for income would give her $70,000 a year, if it was earning 10 percent. (Despite what some financial planners will tell you, it's relatively easy to get an overall return of 10 percent a year. Just make sure a reasonable percentage of your investments is in real estate, where the returns compound because of the leverage effect of borrowing.)

"I've been living very well on about $60,000 a year," Audrey said. "It's good to know that if I wanted to cash in my chips now, I could probably make it."

But Audrey doesn't want to stop working right away. "I love my job and it's exciting to be part of this still-growing company."

Audrey figures that if she went from a sub-zero net worth to one that was more than a million in seven years, she can go from a million to "something more than that" if she applies the same energy and intelligence to her business and investments over the next five years.

Audrey's financial plan for the next five years includes these key elements:

- To save $75,000 a year (the amount she saved last year) for the next five years. Audrey believes this goal will be easy to achieve because (1) both her base compensation and her bonuses will continue to go up as the business grows, and (2) she intends to keep her spending limited. (Total savings for five years would be $375,000.)
- To achieve a 10 percent return on her $75,000-a-year savings by investing, when the time is right, in well-priced real estate and continuing to invest in quality stocks at good prices. The interest gained by compounding annually over five years would increase

her total savings from $375,000 to just over $500,000. This would bring her net worth to $1.6 million.

- To see the value of her company stock double in five years (tracking the anticipated increase in profits). If this happens, it would mean another $375,000.

That would amount to a total net worth of about $2 million, which could give her, at a 10 percent return, a yearly income of $200,000.

"That kind of money would be far more than I would need to pay all my bills, take my vacations, and be happy," Audrey said.

If she chooses this path, she could retire completely by age 55 and cash in her stock. By that time, there is every likelihood that her net worth would be nearly $4 million.

"It seems amazing to me that if I play my cards right—that is to say, if I don't do anything foolish—I could be getting close to $400,000 in passive income every year. Just think of it . . . I'd be 55—still plenty young enough to enjoy myself—with nothing to do all day but relax and spend money!

"The truth is, I know I'll never be able to spend that kind of money . . . but it is fun just thinking about it."

CHAPTER 4

ALAN SILVER*

CONVERTING SELLING SKILLS INTO MILLIONS OF DOLLARS OF EQUITY IN FIVE YEARS

Alan Silver doesn't have an alarm clock. He wakes up when he feels like waking up, usually around eight o'clock. He spends his mornings writing and taking care of business. Afternoons, he does something he enjoys. In the winter, when he's spending time at his second home in Park City, Utah, he skis. Back home in Boca Raton, Florida, he likes to run or jog along the beach, or simply sit by his pool and read.

At 53, Alan is a multimillionaire who does what he wants to do when he wants to do it. But it wasn't always that way.

For 15 years, he made a living selling office supplies. "It was a tough, competitive business," Alan said. "I earned enough money to support my family reasonably well. But it was always a struggle, particularly after the big chains like Office Depot came into the market."

In 1995, Alan had the opportunity to make a switch. He stopped by the office of a friend of his, Rick Walker*, and overheard a conversation that changed his life. Rick, a newsletter publisher, was talking to a vitamin supplier about starting a new company to sell natural supplements to readers of his company's health publication. But he was having a hard time convincing the man that the joint venture would be a good idea.

Rick hung up the phone, frustrated. "Those guys wouldn't recognize a money-making opportunity if it hit them in the head," he said.

"I would," replied Alan. "I mean, I'm a salesman . . . and I'm up for an adventure."

Rick thought about that for a minute. "What do you know about vitamins?" he asked.

"Nothing," Alan admitted.

"And what do you know about the kind of people who read health newsletters?"

"Nothing."

"And what about direct marketing? That's how we sell our newsletters, and that's how we sell products to our subscribers. Do you know how to write advertising copy?"

"No again," said Alan. "But I've got one thing that those other guys don't have. I can recognize a good opportunity when it hits me in the head!"

Alan persuaded Rick to be his mentor as well as his business partner—to teach him enough about the health business to get started, and to personally train him to write advertising copy. The deal was that Alan would draw a small salary to run the vitamin company and, in exchange for putting him into it, funding it, and teaching him the ropes, Rick would share half the profits.

It was a good business deal for both of them—plus it gave both of them the satisfaction of helping a friend.

The plan was for Alan to keep his office supply business going while he and Rick gave the new business a try. "After 15 years of selling pens and pencils to a core group of customers, I could do most of my work on the phone," Alan said. "We figured that if I was willing to work 10 hours a day, I could both keep my old customers happy and start the vitamin company."

The strategy worked. Alan began work early, often at the crack of dawn, and worked late—sometimes till midnight. "I sat my family down before I started and explained to them, 'You're not going to be seeing me much in the coming year.'

"They knew how much I wanted to make the new business work and they were hopeful it could bring us a better life, so they supported me 100 percent. That made that first year tolerable."

Alan came up with a name for his vitamin line, as well as a slogan. "Rick told me that I had a gift for catchy phrases," Alan said. "That boosted my confidence."

Then, Alan sat down to write his first piece of advertising—a four-page flyer that would be inserted into Rick's health newsletter.

"Writing that first letter was a bear," Rick recalled. "Alan had virtually no writing skills and was completely unfamiliar with the concept of direct marketing.

"But he had a well-developed instinct for selling that allowed him to recognize good copy from bad. And he worked tirelessly, rewriting that flyer three or four times. There were moments when I thought he'd give up, but he never did."

Alan's persistence paid off. When the insert was finally done, Rick thought it had a good chance of working.

"I was just happy that—after working so hard on it—I was able to finish a draft that Rick liked," said Alan. "And when it did work, well—that was icing on the cake."

THE PAYOFF

The following month, Alan's flyer was inserted in Rick's health newsletter.

The responses—checks or order forms with credit card information—came in quickly. Because the results were so good, Alan made a deal with another newsletter—run by one of Rick's contacts in the business—to insert the flyer the following month on a 50/50 net, per-response basis. (In other words, Alan's company would split the net revenues with the health newsletter after the money came in and was counted.) And he made a deal with yet another of Rick's contacts to insert the flyer in his newsletter the month after that.

Within six months, Alan's new company had racked up more than a quarter-million dollars in sales. To keep up, he worked extra hours in the evening, helping the people at the fulfillment house fill the orders.

Alan was amazed at how much money was coming in to his little, one-man company. In the first quarter alone, his net profit was $85,000.

"My share of that was $42,500," Alan said. "And I was thrilled. We were pulling in more in a month than I had been making in six months as an office supplier."

Alan's initial euphoria was tempered by an unpleasant reality about fledgling businesses: for the first several years, at least, you have to reinvest all or most of the profits back into the business.

"In the office supply business, I was basically a broker," Alan explained. "My expenses were practically nothing—gas, some client lunches . . . that kind of thing.

"This was a different kind of business altogether. It had much more potential than what I had been doing, but to reach that potential we had to put back in all of the money we were making to spur future growth."

Alan was drawing a salary from the company, but it was only $36,000. "Considering the time I was putting in, that thirty-six grand was like working for minimum wage. On an hourly basis, I would have made out better if I'd been parking cars."

Alan and Rick weren't taking any profits, and sales were increasing. So Alan went to work to develop new products. At the end of the year, the business was doing well enough that it could afford to increase Alan's salary to $44,000 a year. "It wasn't a lot of money, but it was enough to pay the bills," he said.

MAKING THE BIG LEAP—RUNNING YOUR OWN BUSINESS, FULL-TIME

Alan decided to leave the office supply business. Big companies like Office Max and Office Depot were slicing his profit margins and taking away the pride he'd once had in his work.

"It was very distressing, really," Alan said. "It seemed like my customers didn't care anymore about the quality of the products or the good service they were getting from me. All they cared about was getting the best price."

So Alan forged ahead with the vitamin business, full-time. He hired a young woman with some marketing experience to help move the business along, and, with Rick's advice and guidance, the two of them did pretty much everything at first.

"If it was a choice between doing it ourselves or jobbing it out," Alan explained, "we'd do it ourselves because we wanted to learn all the nuts and bolts of the vitamin business. Later on, when things got rolling, we used outside vendors. By that time, we knew what we were doing. Vendors couldn't lie to us about procedures, prices, or deadlines because we knew exactly how the game was played, move by move."

For the first year and a half of operations, the business grew steadily. But then sales leveled off.

"What happened was that we were getting most of our sales through Rick's publishing contacts," Alan said. "In the beginning, we were their only vitamin advertiser. But as time went on, they let other businesses compete with us. We could see the writing on the wall. We knew we had to reach out into the market—go to other media to find new customers."

Advertising to new, unfamiliar markets is always risky. And in Alan's case, it was more complicated because he was so new to the direct-marketing game. With Rick's help, he began the daunting process of creating new advertising packages and testing them out by mailing to a wide range of health, fitness, and supplement lists.

"There's a big difference between promoting a product when you are a recommended vendor, as we were with Rick's publishing contacts, and going out into the vast, unknown marketing world on your own," Alan explained.

"I wasn't sure what sort of products would work best, what kind of pricing to offer, or even how to write a guarantee.

"We did the best we could by reading what the competition was doing and staying close to what we knew was working." (In direct-response advertising, it's pretty easy to identify which ads are working for your competition. They are the ones that keep reappearing in the mail and in magazines and newspapers.) Rick told Alan that "when it comes to breaking into new markets, only crazy people are original."

Despite their best efforts to emulate the success of others, growth was slow during this period. "Rick always said that the most important marketing secrets of every business are invisible to outsiders," said Alan. "I didn't know what he meant by that when I first heard him say it. Now I know."

The invisible secrets of the business Alan had gotten himself into were—like most invisible business secrets—counterintuitive. For example, contrary to what Alan would have predicted, he slowly (and at considerable cost) discovered:

- Most people don't want to understand why they are sick, even if understanding the problem can help them get better. What sick people want are solutions. So it's a waste of your advertising space and your customer's time to explain the problem in detail or at length. State the problem quickly and then devote the majority of your ad and creative energy to explaining the solution.
- The best time to sell a health customer extra supplements is right after he has just bought an adequate supply—in other words, at the precise time he least needs it.
- Men are interested in solving sexual problems more than any other issue, even more serious ones. (But maybe this isn't a counterintuitive secret, after all.)

While learning these secrets, Alan's business was losing money. "Our original strategy—selling our vitamins through flyers inserted in various health newsletters—was still profitable. But we were investing all those profits into expanding into the open market, and that was a process of success by successive failures.

"I was getting advice about what kind of promotions would work best, which products were hot, and which mailing lists would be most responsive to my offers. The advice was well intentioned, but half of it was wrong and that was costing us a lot of money.

"Also, I had two young people working for me by that time, and they were making mistakes. Again, they had the best intentions, but they were inexperienced, just like I was, so it was inevitable that they would make some bad decisions.

"What made matters worse was that I couldn't recognize the mistakes that were being made," Alan said. "It was like trying to play chess without learning what all the pieces were and how they interacted. I didn't know how to play the game."

So Alan decided to downsize so he could stem the negative cash flow and give himself time to learn everything he had to know to run a successful direct-marketing business. He moved the company back into a tiny cubicle and reduced his staff to one person.

DOWNSIZING THE COMPANY, UPGRADING THE SKILLS

To launch the business, Rick had helped Alan write the initial sales copy and get it in front of the right customers. But once they were up and running, Alan was busy in his role as CEO, making the deals and managing the processes. So he'd been delegating the important marketing skills of the business—writing and placing promotional copy—to freelance professionals.

"My first job after downsizing was learning how to write good advertising copy," said Alan. "Luckily, Rick had a friend who is a professional copywriting coach. He agreed to work with me.

"I will never forget the first time I sent him something I'd written. It came back the next day marked up in red pencil. There was more red on that paper than black. It was practically covered in red ink."

Alan's copywriting coach explained that he had two things going for him.

- He was a great natural salesman.
- He wrote like a sixth grader.

Alan was understandably taken aback by that second point. But then his coach explained that writing simply is a great advantage in the world of advertising. "The promises and claims are what count in copy, he told me. Not the adverbs and adjectives."

Step by step, Alan mastered the basics of advertising to the health market, always trying to keep his writing simple enough for a sixth grader to understand. "For me," said Alan, "that was the key to writing strong copy."

Rick put Alan in contact with another person who could help him—an expert in determining which mailing lists would be most profitable for a particular type of business. Alan followed his advice and saw a gradual increase in his results.

Alan was learning how important expert help is in breaking into a new market. He made it a point to get to know more experts, both on a professional and social basis.

"I realized that a lot of my future success depended on how good my Rolodex was," he said. "And with my background in sales, I wasn't shy about introducing myself to new people.

"Another important lesson I learned back then was that there's an advantage to working cooperatively with your competitors. I had been schooled to think that my competitors were my enemies, but I soon came to realize that many of them can be your best friends."

Alan's business profited from several key list-exchange deals he made with other, fast-growing health marketing companies. "This strategy worked well," he said. "At one time, it accounted for more than half of our profits."

To keep coming up with new ideas for the copy he was writing, Alan did a lot of research—and in the process, learned a lot about nutrition and its effect on health. This proved invaluable when he met professionals in the natural health business, especially doctors and research scientists. Impressed with Alan's knowledge, they were very comfortable dealing with him.

Alan found that his growing technical knowledge really paid off when he was ready to take the next step in building his business. To add credibility to his products and his company, he decided to find a doctor who would endorse his formulations and help him come up with new ones.

"I didn't want to settle for just any guy in a white jacket who would sign his name in exchange for money," Alan said. "I wanted to make a deal with a research-oriented doctor who practiced natural medicine on a daily basis.

"The doctor I teamed up with was a very serious guy who wanted to make a serious name for himself," Alan explained. "Before he would agree to do business with me, he wanted to meet me and find out about my commitment to quality products.

"When he realized I could talk the talk, he was convinced," explained Alan. "We made a deal and that deal has been working well for both of us ever since."

DIFFERENTIATING YOURSELF FROM
THE COMPETITION

One of Alan's core strategies was to create products that would set him apart from his competition. After trying various approaches, he met with the doctor and Rick, and the three of them decided that the company's niche should be high-end, high-quality supplements.

"It was a risky strategy, because high quality meant high costs," Alan explained. "And I have to admit, I was scared at first that I would end up losing the modest profit margin I was living on because of the increased costs."

But the strategy worked. Alan's advertising copy now emphasized the superior quality of his products—and the response rate increased significantly. "We were all very happy when we saw those early, positive returns. It meant that we could afford to sell our customers the highest-quality supplements—supplements that were measurably better than those of many of our competitors. And this meant, we believed, more back-end sales. A satisfied customer is one who will buy from you over and over again."

Aided by better advertising copy, better list selection, the strength of a doctor's endorsement, and better quality products, profits were once again growing.

"It felt so good to see the sales and profits climbing back up again after that one bad year," Alan said. "When we bypassed our previous best month in sales, we all celebrated. Not only had we broken our sales record, we had achieved record profits at the same time."

Since Alan wanted his company to continue to enjoy its upward arc, he made a promise to himself: he'd make sure his customer service was top notch. "I called my staff together and congratulated them for what they had done so far. Then I explained my customer service goals.

"I told them that I never wanted a single customer to be ignored. I wanted every question, every complaint, and every suggestion to be carefully considered. I knew that if I didn't treat my customers like gold, they would eventually find their way over to my competitors. And I also suspected that if we listened to their complaints and suggestions, we'd find out all sorts of valuable things about how to make our business better."

The company's revival continued steadily and happily for three years. Then Alan came up with a new product—one that was really different.

It was a multivitamin packaged in an aluminum canister. Because many people take five or six different vitamins every day, he got the idea to create something that would minimize the fuss and hassle of dealing with all those bottles. So he introduced a cellophane packet of six essential vitamins—which was, at the time, a novelty. You'd just open the canister and grab one packet in the morning and one in the evening. Very convenient.

"That one product promotion alone brought in sales of three million dollars," Alan said. "At the end of that year—only four and a half years after I quit my job and got into the supplement business full-time—I was able to look at my bank balance and see that I had saved my first million dollars!"

If Alan had been satisfied with having a million-dollar nest egg, he could have put the business on cruise control, paid his living expenses with his salary, and worked part-time. Instead, he decided to double his efforts for a few years so he could stop working entirely one day.

"Because of my background in selling office supplies," Alan said, "I understood a fundamental principle of retail sales: the more product you put on the shelf, the more you sell."

Alan was running a direct-marketing company, not an office supply store . . . but the same principle applied. By continuing to put money back into the business, he was able to make the company stronger and even more successful.

THE WISE DECISIONS OF A WEALTH BUILDER

As the company grew, Alan's personal expenses remained the same. Although he could easily afford to buy a huge house, he stayed in his smallish town home. And while some of his colleagues were driving Porsches and BMWs, he tooled around in a mid-level Infiniti. He lived well and he lived comfortably, but he didn't spend anywhere near what he could afford to spend.

"I never felt the need to advertise my wealth," Alan said. "It was better for me to put my profits into savings and let them mount."

Alan continued to live on a very modest budget. He said, "I've bought my share of toys in recent years, but I'm still basically the same guy. Give me a nice bottle of wine and a good friend to talk to and I'm where I want to be."

Meanwhile, his fortune grew so large that his financial planner had to persuade him to make some changes for tax-saving and asset-protection purposes.

These days, Alan gives back to his family and friends. "I spend some money on myself. And I enjoy it. But it's very important to me that my family and friends are taken care of, too."

Alan's wealth is divided between personal real estate, commercial real estate, and very conservative investments.

His conservative bent was influenced by his father, who was a man of the Depression. So Alan has the lion's share of his money in municipal bonds and CDs (which he's careful not to extend too far out in case interest rates change), as well as growth funds.

And he has a small, six-figure sum in a conservative stock-management account.

Alan's approach to investing is the same as his father's: a penny saved is a penny earned. Collect enough pennies, and you'll have a dollar. Enough dollars, and pretty soon you'll be rich.

A while back, Alan set a goal to retire at age 55. As 55 creeps up on him, he realizes that he doesn't want to retire, because he's having too much fun. He enjoys making money and he enjoys the business he's in.

His schedule is much more relaxed now than it was when he started the business. He spends most of his mornings at home, drinking coffee and reading the newspaper by the pool. By the time he gets into the office at 11:00, his staff has put in a half-day's work. He spends part of his afternoon reviewing reports with his key people and the other half writing advertising copy. "I'm still my company's best copywriter," Alan said. "And that says a lot, because we have some pretty good guys writing for us."

He is away from the office—either at his home in Park City or some other vacation spot—about 10 days per month. And he has no problem taking off to celebrate one of his daughters' birthdays, go fishing with friends, or attend a family reunion.

"My lifestyle now is unbeatable. I work just enough to keep myself happy and challenged. And the rest of my time is devoted to having fun. The bottom line is that I'm very content.

"Real wealth," he said, "is feeling like you're happy with what you have and you're not worried about the future. That's how I feel. I really enjoy the people I work with and I'm very glad that I can take care of the people I love. And the best thing is, I don't need that darn alarm clock any more.

"If that's not the definition of wealth," he said, "I don't know what is."

HOW ALAN BECAME A MULTIMILLIONAIRE
IN LESS THAN FIVE YEARS

Alan's story is an interesting one because, unlike most of the other people profiled for this book, he was (a) a self-employed businessman with (b) a sales-oriented business when he came to the conclusion that he needed to make a change.

For 15 years, he had owned and ran an office supply company that catered to small businesses. He understood the basics of business, including the dynamics of supply and demand, the importance of cost containment, the necessity of good customer service, and, most of all, the art of selling. "I've been selling stuff since I was a kid," he explained. "My father, who sold junk at one time to support the family, was my first teacher."

Most people who dream about becoming millionaires are handicapped by an ignorance of business and a fear of selling, but Alan was comfortable and experienced in both arenas.

"The problem for me," he said, "was that the industry I had chosen, the office supply business, experienced a massive change."

Spurred by the huge success of stores like Costco and Home Depot, venture capitalists started investing big dollars into mega-stores in the office supply industry. As office managers discovered they could save lots of money while getting a better selection and better payment terms from the larger suppliers, small operations like Alan's were gradually choked out of existence.

Many of Alan's competitors vainly tried to hold on or survive by specializing. But Alan recognized early on that his prospects were limited, and opted to make a change while business was still good enough to provide him with an income during his transition.

This is an important principle of what I call "chicken entrepreneurship" (the only start-your-own-business strategy I recommend): since you can't know if your brilliant new business idea will work out until you've given it a good test for a year or two, don't quit your day job.

Alan began his quest for a new business the way good salesmen look for new clients: by asking everyone he knew for leads. Making that initial connection with Rick was part luck (it was fortuitous that Alan was there when Rick was talking to someone about needing a vitamin supplier)—but he had already told Rick several times that he was looking to make a change.

"If Alan hadn't been there that day," Rick said, "I probably would have asked him if he wanted to try it. I knew he was looking for a new business. Sooner or later, I would have come up with something for him."

Too often, capable people are reluctant to reach out. Pride, shame, and fear sometimes prevent us from doing the smart thing: letting our friends and colleagues know that we need help. Alan didn't have that problem. He knew from his many years as a salesman that asking for simple favors is a powerful way to create success. He had a great deal of success in his early years just by asking existing customers if they could recommend someone else he could sell to.

"When I first starting asking, I sometimes felt a little embarrassed about what I was doing," Alan said. "After all, this person had just been kind enough to place an order with me. What right did I have to take his money and then ask him if he had any friends or acquaintances who would give me their money, too?"

What Alan came to realize is that asking for help—if done honestly and without applying pressure to the other person—is like giving a gift. Wealthy and successful people are usually happy to support others who are just starting out, because it gives them the sense that they are paying back the universe for their own good fortune.

ASKING FOR HELP

Before you attempt to launch a new business, make a list of everyone you know who could possibly help you. Begin with any friends or colleagues who are successful at business or have some specific (legal/financial) knowledge about business that will be useful to you.

Make appointments with each of these people and tell them, over a meal that you have paid for, that you value their opinion . . . that you have decided to go into business . . . and that you are "hoping to get their counsel" on one or two important issues.

POWER-CHARGE YOUR NETWORKING

Networking is the perfect way to build a support group or find a mentor, your next superstar employee, or a deal that could be worth millions.

Andrew Gordon, the financial editor of my *Early to Rise* e-zine, knows from personal experience how profitable networking can be.

In 1997, Andrew befriended a 16-year-old kid at an environmental trade show in Singapore. The kid loved hanging around Andrew's booth, so Andrew gave him free passes so he could continue to visit every day.

That kid is now a 25-year-old doctor with a thriving practice in India. In 2005, he put Andrew in touch with his uncle. Two months later, Andrew had a $1.2 million environmental project near Mumbai.

Sometimes networking is as easy as giving away a few free tickets. At other times, you may have to work a little harder—maybe even do something brazen and calculating, such as sending a gift along with a personal letter.

A few years ago, I was the subject of such a transparent and disreputable effort—and it worked.

That morning, my assistant stuffed my mailbox with letters, bills, faxes, publications, and interoffice memos. But she personally handed me a package, because it was bigger and evidently more valuable than the rest of the mail.

I opened it right away. (The mail waited and waited.) It contained a large, colorful book: *Buzan's Book of Genius,* by Tony Buzan and Raymond Keane. It was the oddest thing. "Who could have sent me this?" I wondered.

I found the answer in an enclosed letter. The book was from someone I had met in London, an attendee at a speech I'd given on productivity. He'd taken the time, I remembered, to introduce himself to me then.

I might have forgotten about him completely were it not for this gift.

I glanced through the book, thinking, "This must have cost this guy a lot of money," and I promised myself I'd read it.

In his enclosed letter, he made reference to our earlier meeting and his subsequent reading of *ETR.* And he said he thought I'd enjoy the book because it covers some of the concerns I've focused on in *ETR* and in my consulting work.

How could I not be pleased?

> A few days later, I zipped through the book and did, indeed, find material there that I could use.
>
> As a consequence, this young man now has a first-name relationship with me that might, one day in the future, be a considerable benefit to him.
>
> What about you? Is there someone you know, but not well, that you'd like to know better? Have you met someone recently with whom you'd like to become more familiar?
>
> Take a chance by sending a gift. I recommend books, because they have the right balance between personal and impersonal and are both useful and reasonably priced.
>
> You never know what valuable contacts you can make with your generosity.

Be frank with them about your plans, and ask them every possible question you can think of. Pay close attention to what they say. Take notes. When they say something you find particularly helpful or informative, acknowledge it.

At the end of the meeting, but before they stand up, thank them sincerely and ask them to give you the names and phone numbers of anyone they know who could fill you in on other aspects of business in general or the industry you've chosen. Don't let them get away without giving you at least one name and phone number. A half-dozen is what you are shooting for.

By attempting to get a half-dozen names from everyone on your contact list, you will quickly build up a very substantial support group for your new project. Even if your initial list consists of only two people and you collect only two names from each of them, your network will expand amazingly fast. Two becomes four . . . four becomes eight . . . eight becomes 16 . . . 16 becomes 32 . . . 32 becomes 64 . . . and so on.

Of course, you'll never have to go that far. Before you've had meetings with two dozen people, you will have learned tons—maybe even everything you need to be successful in your new business. More important, you'll have connected with several successful and/or influential people who will want to see you succeed. At least one or two of them will be willing to help you, just as Rick was willing to help Alan.

RIDING ON COATTAILS

Alan's initial success in the vitamin business came from his relationship with Rick. To generate extra, back-end revenues for his publishing business, Rick was looking for a nutritional supplement company that would be willing to invest in a direct-marketing campaign and target the readers of his health newsletter. When some of the larger vitamin businesses seemed reluctant to get involved in a new market they didn't understand, Alan had the opportunity he had been looking for. With Rick's assistance, he formed a little company with the express purpose of selling a single product (multivitamins) to a single marketplace (the publishing company's subscribers).

Because there was a mutual need—the publishing company's need for additional back-end revenue and Alan's need to start a new business—it was relatively easy for the two men to agree on a joint venture that would limit the initial marketing costs and risks for both parties.

Alan would provide the product and pay to have the orders fulfilled. Rick's publishing company would provide free access to its customers and even cover the printing costs of the inserted advertisement. With the costs and risks limited, each party was willing to do its part of the venture. And when the initial test results proved positive, each party was willing to reinvest its profits to expand the business.

Another principle of chicken entrepreneurship is that 50 percent of a sure thing is a much better bet than 100 percent of a long shot. That's what the insert advertising deal was for Alan: the chance to launch his business with limited risk and a very good chance of succeeding.

Any time you market a horizontal product on a back-end basis (in other words, any time you sell a related product to a recently acquired customer), your chances of success are 80 percent or better. Although Rick could have been mistaken in his decision to sell vitamins and other natural supplements to readers of his health newsletter, his level of confidence was high because he understood this basic law of advertising.

The deal that Rick set up for Alan is the kind of deal any smart chicken entrepreneur should look for. Before you invest lots of money in your first pedal-to-the-metal marketing campaign, stop and ask yourself, "Is there any business out there that will let me try out my products and promotions on a back-end, shared-risk basis?"

Finding suitable candidates for coattail marketing should begin the way networking for ideas and support begins: by making a list of the businesses and media outlets that service the industry you are going into. This is usually no more difficult than getting on the Internet and locating a trade organization that services that industry. But if that path doesn't lead you where you need to go, you can assemble a list of candidates, one at a time, by making phone calls and requesting "informational" interviews.

In attempting to make joint-venture marketing deals, avoid corporate salespeople. They are the most likely to be willing to talk to you, but the least likely to cut a joint-venture deal. They see your interest in their business as a sign that you are willing to spend some money with them. They want your commission. Any time you give them will probably be frustrating and costly because, being salespeople, they will be better at selling *you* than you will be at selling *them*.

Get in contact with product managers, profit center managers, and, if possible, company owners. They are in a position to see the advantages of a longer-term, joint-venture relationship with an aggressive new business.

Sell them on the idea that, by linking up with you, they can create a new revenue stream for themselves without taking on the burden of running a new business. Experienced business managers know that new product lines are time-consuming and difficult. If you can convince them that they can enjoy a steady stream of future income without the hassles and risks of getting into something new, chances are they will go for it.

Be prepared when you are making such presentations. Come with concrete benefits, impressive stats, and—most important—blow their minds with off-the-wall financial projections. Admit that the numbers you are showing them are "purely conjectural." But point out how lovely it would be if they came true.

If you get one coattail deal, look for another. If you get two, look for a third. Joint-venture deals are enormously helpful to growing businesses, because they simplify operations and dramatically reduce cash flow requirements.

Alan's initial success with his new business was due to two factors:

- Winning himself a support team of experts who set him on the right path, and
- Making a coattail joint venture with a successful health publisher

But if that was all he did, his business would have probably failed—because that one good relationship with Rick's newsletter business wasn't big enough to keep his company growing. One relationship seldom is. And when it is—when your business is dependent on a single client—your future wealth and peace of mind are in the hands of a business that you can't control.

Coattail relationships are great for launching your business and, as I said earlier, the more of them you can make, the better. Your cash flow will be more stable and your chances of making other, ancillary marketing deals will increase.

But if you want to take your business to another level, one that offers you a chance to direct your own growth, you need to take the step that Alan took: developing a promotional campaign to generate, on a cost-effective basis, new customers by selling something in the open market.

FINDING THE GOLDEN KEY TO YOUR FUTURE WEALTH

The basis of every business, large or small, is sales. Generally speaking, there are two kinds of sales:

- The first sale—the one that turns a prospect into a customer.
- All other sales—what we in the direct-marketing industry call back-end sales.

Back-end sales create (or should create) most of your profits. This is because back-end response rates are generally much higher and sales costs are much lower. Although many businesses don't maximize the enormous potential of marketing to the back end, the best and most successful companies become masterful at it.

Alan's coattail relationship with a health publisher was essentially a back-end marketing operation. The primary relationship was between the health publisher and its customers. By being positioned in its publication on a preferential basis, Alan's products enjoyed a tacit endorsement. That advantage was the reason response rates were always positive and initial profits were so high. And since Alan didn't know any better at the time, it was why he was initially very optimistic about his early promotions and surprised when his business gradually stalled.

When you have a coattail deal, you must remember that the person wearing the coat is always in charge. And if he or she feels like you are getting too good a deal, they have the power to curtail your sales, reduce your share, or cut you out entirely.

Alan got beyond this problem by recognizing the possibility early on, and turning his efforts to launching a new product that would sell effectively in the open market.

What wouldn't work, he realized, was his multivitamin packets. There were simply too many multivitamin products in the marketplace already. Alan's innovative packaging just didn't have enough sex appeal to compete efficiently in that super-competitive world.

Developing an efficient front-end product is the most important task of any business builder. The most important and also most difficult.

When entrepreneurs come into an industry for the first time, they often bring with them ideas for "breakthrough" products. Most of these ideas, when tested, turn out to be complete duds.

There is a good reason for that—but it's one that is, as far as I know, never discussed in business books or courses. As I said earlier, every industry has a half-dozen or so core sales and marketing secrets that are invisible to the outside world. Suffice it to say that the reason most great new ideas fail is because those ideas are based on what the industry looks like from the outside, and outsiders only see what's visible.

There is no easy way to discover the invisible secrets of any industry, unless you have the advice of an industry insider. (But beware— many of these secrets mutate over time, so make sure your expert is a current expert.)

Fortunately for Alan, he had great mentors who pointed him in the right direction when it came to product and promotion ideas. But none of them were in-the-trenches experts, so they could not tell him, "Just do this and it will work." Like most new business owners, Alan was forced to fly on a wing and a prayer.

After gathering the best advice he could, he wrote and tested several front-end promotions in three health areas that his research indicated were active and growing: joint pain, prostate-related problems, and erectile dysfunction.

"Other than the occasional bout with tennis elbow," Alan said, "I had no familiarity with any of these problems. But the data said that baby boomers were buying natural remedies to combat them. If that was where the business was, I figured I'd better get myself up to speed on them."

Alan spent a few hours every day researching medical studies online, reading press reports, and, when he could find them, studying promotions for products to treat these three health issues. "Before that, if you had told me that one day I would know what dihydrotestosterone (DHT) was and how to pronounce it, I would have told you that you were smoking the wrong kind of cigarettes. But since my business depended on it, I had to learn it."

Term by term, Alan learned about these conditions and the natural remedies that were helpful in dealing with them. And word by word, he learned how to write about them.

Because he had a close working relationship with a doctor who was an expert in natural medicine, he was able to develop three state-of-science formulations that he was excited to write about.

Despite all his hard work, success wasn't immediate. "We had some good returns, but we also had our losers. It was a slow, deliberate process of testing and waiting for results and then testing again," Alan said. "Getting something new that works in the general market isn't easy. But if you keep at it—and learn from your mistakes—you will eventually get your breakthrough."

Alan's breakthrough came after more than six months of testing. The winner was a product to prevent and treat prostate problems—a combination of several natural ingredients which, though proven in clinical tests, were largely unknown by the market. And Alan's formula was produced in a way that made it possible for the bloodstream to absorb those ingredients quickly—a "revolutionary delivery system," his advertising called it.

By the time Alan had figured out how to make that product work, he had accumulated enough knowledge to make his other two products work. "Gradually, I discovered the secrets of how to win over new customers in the natural health market," he said. "It was a tough, competitive business at the time. Now, it's even tougher."

When asked for his secrets, Alan replied: "I'll be happy to give them to you after you've bought my business. But right now, I'm really liking what I'm doing, so I don't think you have enough money to buy me out."

Finding the secret selling tricks and techniques of a new business requires expert advice, probing research, and diligent follow-through. It also requires a lot of cash. Most businesses that fail (as most new businesses do) do so because they don't have the cash to sustain themselves during this period—the period of discovering the invisible selling secrets.

That's another reason why coattail deals and joint-venture marketing agreements are so useful, if you can get them. They give you a nice, steady flow of back-end generated cash that you can reinvest in figuring out how to make your front-end marketing work.

MASTERING THE MEGA-POWER OF THE BACK END

Once you get your front end working, the back end—by comparison—is a piece of cake. The secret to making back-end marketing work is to recognize the natural curve of enthusiasm that is part of every sales transaction and to design your back-end selling strategy to take full advantage of it.

When a prospect responds to your sales message, something important happens. For a certain period of time, he lives in a heightened state of expectation. Because of the emotional messages that are now implanted in his brain, every time he sees your product, hears your company's name, or sees your logo, he will experience certain hopes, feelings, and desires that—if you do your job properly—will result in additional sales.

Although most people want to think of themselves as rational beings who buy for sensible reasons, the truth is that most sales transactions are emotional events designed to trigger thoughts and impulses that are fundamentally irrational—if not downright foolish.

- "If I buy that sports car, I will be more attractive to good-looking women."
- "If I buy that vacuum cleaner, I will prove (to myself and my friends) that I am a very good housekeeper."
- "If I buy that new diet book, I will once and for all lose that extra 30 pounds and feel good about myself."

One of the many interesting things about the psychology of buying is the curious fact that one emotionally charged, irrational buying decision will usually lead to another, similar one . . . and then another . . . and another one after that. This pattern of multiple, often unnecessary, purchases is typical of almost every sort of buying transaction, from diet books to cosmetics to health products and even cars.

How many times have you, after running out and buying a watch or a pair of shoes or a video, made a second or a third such purchase a short time later?

Have you ever developed a passion for a sport or hobby? And if so, did you ever find yourself buying everything you could find connected with your newfound passion—even products you had neither the time nor the interest to use?

I doubt that any product or service is exempt. Not toilet paper. Not diapers. Not plastic surgery.

This impulsive spending spree that follows the first purchase is what I call the "buying frenzy." It's very important to understand this phenomenon, because it allows you—as a marketer or entrepreneur—to take advantage of your easiest and most profitable potential sales. If you make the commonsense mistake of thinking that one 85-foot schooner is enough for one man, you are making a very serious error.

Some buying frenzies last longer than others. Some are more intense. Generally, the less time that's available, the more frequent these purchases need to be. And buying frenzies vary in duration and intensity, depending on the type of purchase. A model-airplane buying frenzy is different from a spiritual-enlightenment buying frenzy.

To capitalize on buying frenzies, keep the following in mind:

- You must know your market to understand the pattern of your customers' frenzy.

- Buying frenzies end only if one of two things happens: (1) your customer runs out of money or credit, or (2) you stop selling.
- Your buying frenzy customer will not be satisfied with the first purchase. He will need to buy more to get the same emotional charge. If you don't satisfy that desire, your competitor will.
- The length and duration of frenzy purchases are determined by factors you can and should understand. Pay attention to them and you will be able to create a follow-up selling campaign that will give your customer everything she wants and make your bottom line fatter.

After Alan figured out how to bring in new customers at a "breakeven" (meaning that the revenue was equal to or less than the cost of acquiring the customer), he got to work developing an effective back-end marketing program.

"I knew from my experience working with Rick's health publishing company that back-end sales are low risk and high profit," said Alan. "When my own customer file grew from just a few dozen names to hundreds and then to thousands, I knew it would be only a matter of time before I figured out how to monetize those names."

Alan developed a series of back-end direct-mail promotions that (a) attempted to get his new customers to order a second or third batch of whatever it was they had just ordered, (b) gave the new customers a chance to join a "discount club" to make future purchases, and (c) sold them—in fairly rapid order—a series of formulations for everything from improved eyesight to stress relief.

"I eventually put together a catalog that featured all our latest and hottest products, and sent it to my customer file twice a month. It proved to be the best thing we did on the back end," Alan said. "Our profit margins were unbelievable."

Once the front end and back end were in place and working smoothly, Alan was in a position to test out other ways to boost his business—secondary ways that were relatively easy and added nicely to his bottom line.

One of these was to develop relationships with his competitors. Most businesspeople have an antagonistic view of competition and treat their competitors accordingly. But Alan tried a very different approach: sharing and cooperating with his competitors in an effort to expand his market.

"When your company sells everything that it has to your customer list, that list becomes gradually weaker," Alan explained. "They've seen everything you have over and over again. If they haven't bought something from you after you've hit them 10 or 20 times, chances are they aren't going to respond to you in the future. But that doesn't mean they won't respond to an offer from one of your competitors."

Alan made several list-swapping and joint-marketing deals with a few of his chief competitors, and they all worked out very well for him. "When I make deals like this, I always try to make it reciprocal," Alan said. "That way, even if my products aren't selling to a competitor's list, I'm still making money off the list I swapped with him. So the more names a competitor brings in, the more that competitor will give me for helping him out."

Extra bonus: by exchanging lists with one or two competitors, you can also saturate each others' lists before another competitor has the chance to tempt your customers with his products.

TREAT YOUR SUPERSTARS RIGHT

One thing Alan learned that helped him avoid a lot of growing pains was the importance of finding good employees and treating them well. "Since I wasn't an expert in my business when I started, I knew I had to surround myself with very good people who could help me avoid making mistakes," he said.

"It took me a while to hire my first marketing assistant. And when I finally found the right person, I knew I had to make her happy by treating her right. She was smart, very hardworking, and extremely loyal. She was strong enough to grow with the business as it got bigger. I felt sure she could keep up with the growing demand—and I was right."

By taking extra time to hire only the best people and outsourcing work that could be outsourced, Alan managed to grow his business from a few hundred thousand dollars a year to almost $10 million with only three employees. "Friends and colleagues thought my office was a front for some kind of illegal activity," Alan laughed. "They couldn't believe that I could do that kind of business with just myself and three ladies."

HOW TO HELP YOUR EMPLOYEES DO THEIR BEST WORK

As an entrepreneur, you're likely to be a go-to person—someone who always has the answer to questions . . . who can always explain things . . . who can always get problems solved. This is a good and a bad thing. Good because it gives you power. Bad because it can stifle your employees— and, in the process, overwhelm you with extra work.

One thing that happens frequently is what I call "reverse delegation." This is when a subordinate asks for your help in doing something, and you wind up agreeing to do it yourself. Big mistake.

Another very common trap is what I call the Mr. Solution Syndrome. This is when you get into the habit of proudly solving every problem that's put before you. You are so good, so smart . . . you believe you can do it all. Like reverse delegation, this robs your employees of the opportunity to learn how to solve problems themselves.

The answer? Simple. Next time a subordinate asks you what to do about a problem, tell him to come back with three reasonable solutions and you'll choose the best one together.

This has several benefits.

1. It abbreviates the interruption and lets you get back to work.
2. It encourages the employee to think for himself—a good long-term investment in developing business skills.
3. The process may lead to a better solution than either of you would have come up with alone.

When your business is growing fast, there is a strong temptation to hire people quickly to fill real or imagined work needs. Keeping a balance between how many employees you really need and how many you can afford is much easier if you pick only the most ambitious and talented people to work for you.

You, too, can build a successful business if you follow Alan's path. Keep his journey in mind, and you might end up a multimillion-dollar success in a few short years.

CHAPTER 5

BRUCE BUFFER

GIVING UP A SIX-FIGURE INCOME TO GENERATE A SEVEN-FIGURE NET WORTH

Making money was never a problem for Bruce Buffer. In 1975, at the young age of 18, he got his first job at a national telemarketing company. His job was selling office supplies, and within two weeks he was the number one salesman in the 50-person company. In his third month, he was promoted to sales manager.

"I was, by far, the youngest person in that office," Bruce said. "It must have been tough for some of the older guys to report to a teenager."

By the end of his first year, Bruce's commission income was around $50,000. "And at that time, 50 grand was a lot of money!"

Bruce's commissions were substantial, but he could see that the profits he was making for the company were many times what he was making. "I worked for them for a while," he said. "But then my entrepreneurial spirit took over and—after I had figured out how the business was run from the top down—I quit and started my own business as a competitor."

When Bruce left, many of the company's best salespeople followed him. The exodus created a commotion, and the commotion resulted in a lawsuit. "One moment, I was a model entrepreneur," Bruce remembered. "The next moment, I was fighting a million-dollar lawsuit.

"I didn't have the money or the know-how to deal with it. I resisted for a while, because I didn't think there was anything wrong with what I was doing. But the pressure was too great, and I stopped fighting."

The company agreed to withdraw the suit if Bruce would come back and work for them. "I realized that the entire lawsuit was just a ploy to get me back. So I negotiated a pretty good deal."

To lure him back, his former employer agreed to reimburse Bruce for his legal fees, double his salary, and give him a bonus. Bruce continued to work for them . . . and eventually became a partner.

"That lasted a while," said Bruce. "But then the entrepreneurial bug bit me again. When I left this time, I started a completely different kind of company, selling and installing high-tech alarm and camera systems for retail businesses, corporations, and homes."

At about the same time, he got involved with a company that had him travel around the country to speak about business opportunities in the health industry. And to keep himself busy on weekends, he invested in real estate and collectibles, and "dabbled in" the import-export business.

EASY PROFITS LEAD TO EASY SPENDING

All of these ventures—and his investments—provided Bruce with a steady stream of cash that paid for a luxurious lifestyle. "I have never hesitated to spend money on myself and my family. I like to live well. I can't deny it."

Bruce rationalized his extravagance by telling himself (and anyone who questioned him), "Buying what I want motivates me to make more."

Yet, as he got older, he realized that his profligate spending was working against him. "Living like a rich person is one thing. Being rich is something else."

Bruce was making a good income, but he was saving very little of it. "I had money in the stock market and I had lots of valuable collectibles, but I also had a good deal of debt. I never stopped to calculate my net worth at the time—but if I had, I am sure I would have been disappointed."

When his stock portfolio got crushed by the high-tech bust, he faced a financial truth that some high-income earners never fully understand: wealth is not determined by how much you can spend but by how much you can save.

"Suddenly, I began to see wealth in a completely different light," Bruce said. "I still liked spending money, but I learned to enjoy saving it, too. I adopted a completely different mind-set about what it means to be rich. It was no longer about cars and boats and expensive dinners. It was about college for the kids and retirement funds."

Bruce's financial goals changed accordingly. Whereas he once fueled his ambitions with dreams of new sports cars and vintage movie posters, he now visualized his various bank and investment accounts growing larger.

"It's ironic. When I was motivated by spending, I was pretty satisfied with the high income I was earning. But when I started to think in terms of saving, my income goals changed. I began dreaming of ways to increase my income radically so I could put most of it into investments and savings."

That was in 1993. What happened next was a mixture of circumstance, shrewd marketing skills, and the ability to recognize a once-in-a-lifetime opportunity.

RECOGNIZING THE POTENTIAL FOR COLOSSAL WEALTH

Bruce's half-brother, Michael Buffer, had been a ring announcer for boxing matches for many years. Having established himself at the top of the game, he then trademarked his signature phrase: "Let's Get Ready to Rumble®."

"I had always admired Michael—and I'd been handling some aspects of his career for a while," said Bruce. "But inspiration struck when I saw him live in Vegas, announcing the classic Riddick Bowe / Evander Holyfield match.

"When I heard how that crowd of 15,000 people roared when he kicked off the fight with his 'Let's Get Ready to Rumble®,' a lightbulb went off in my head. I could see how much more he could do with that great phrase. I realized he could eventually become a household name. And I knew that if he would let me, I could help him become not only the most famous sports announcer in the world, but a world-famous announcer for all kinds of entertainment spectacles."

Bruce persuaded Michael to let him push full speed ahead. "I told him I had two goals: first, to make Let's Get Ready to Rumble®, the most recognized and successful trademark phrase in sports and entertainment history, and, second, to make him richer and more famous than he ever dreamed.

"Of course, I intended to add to my own wealth in the process."

Bruce and Michael formalized their deal in 1994. At that time, Michael was announcing primarily for boxing events. But within three years, he was announcing for all sorts of other sports, too, including the NBA, the NFL, WCW Wrestling, the NHL, the Indy 500, NASCAR, the MLB World Series, bass fishing, and even championship tennis. Michael also began appearing in movies and on television shows, and made personal appearances at various corporate events.

Bruce realized that his half-brother's income from live appearances, though good, was limited by Michael's time. So he had to come up with other ways to market him that were based on Michael's "brand." The first such program allowed sports teams, businesses, and even wealthy private individuals to use personalized audio recordings by Michael to kick off their events, promote their products, or celebrate special occasions such as birthdays, bar mitzvahs, and weddings.

"You would be amazed at some of the inventive ways we found to let Michael perform his magic," Bruce said.

Once the audio-recording business was up and running, Bruce turned his attention to licensing the Let's Get Ready to Rumble® trademark brand. "In the beginning, I had to break down a lot of barriers," said Bruce. "But I was determined to succeed, because I knew that Michael's brand was strong enough to reach a much wider demographic than the one that followed boxing. I didn't want to abandon his core market, and we never did. But I also wanted to put him in center court for the NBA Championships and on the 50-yard line for the NFL Championship games. And I wanted to put his brand on toys, video games, and many other products.

"So I kept pushing and pushing . . . and once people started to understand the power of the brand and how it could be used in different situations, business started to snowball."

By 1999, five years after Bruce and Michael made their deal, the Buffer partnership had grossed over $400 million in retail sales for its licensees.

EXPANDING THE MONEY-MAKING UNIVERSE

Motivated by his newfound desire to develop a seven-figure net worth, Bruce kept looking for additional income opportunities. One came to him as a result of successfully promoting his half-brother's franchise.

It was 1996. Bruce had just signed Michael to an exclusive deal with the WCW Wrestling League. It was a very lucrative deal, but it prevented Michael from working for other, similar events. One of the events Michael was prohibited from announcing at was the Ultimate Fighting Championship (UFC), a mixed martial arts tournament.

"If my brother couldn't do it, I thought, 'Well, maybe I can.' " Within a year, Bruce had negotiated his own deal with the UFC to be the permanent "Voice of the UFC Octagon."

That was 11 years ago. Since then, the UFC has become widely known throughout the world—and so has Bruce as the voice of both the UFC Octagon and the sport of mixed martial arts.

"I have made a lot of money with the UFC and by marketing my brother's brand," Bruce said. "But even with that huge income, I didn't start to build real wealth until 1994. The big change happened when I made the decision to make saving my top priority.

"I can't tell you exactly, but if I had to guess I'd say that I accumulated my first million about four years after I made that mental transformation. Since then, of course, I've been adding to my wealth. Nowadays, saving is such an ingrained habit, I don't think much about it."

A MILLION-DOLLAR LIFESTYLE

Bruce's commitment to saving and investing hasn't affected his lifestyle. He drives a Mercedes, lives by the beach in Marina Del Rey, owns a $2 million home in Malibu, and has an ideal schedule.

"I have no set hours," said Bruce. "I manage my time well and do whatever it takes to succeed, even if that means working seven days a week. When you enjoy what you do, it isn't work, it's a way of life.

"I could be going to work in Vegas, or I could be flying to Sweden or Japan on a Wednesday and flying back home by Monday. Then I could have a UFC to announce the next Saturday.

"It can get crazy, but it's always exciting, always fun, and I can take the day off whenever I want to or need to. I'm constantly meeting successful people and creating deals and ventures for my brother and our brand. With e-mail and a phone, I can do business anywhere in the world and never slack off or leave a stone unturned."

Bruce hired a personal assistant, Kristen, who has made his life much easier. (In fact, she is so good at her job that she was promoted to vice president of Buffer Enterprises, Inc.) Because Kristen is there to take care of anything that comes up, Bruce no longer worries when he has to be out of the office for long periods of time.

"It's crucial to hire great people who share your dream," Bruce said. "Kristen is worth her weight in gold, and Michael and I are blessed to have her as our V.P. Whether handling important business affairs or just answering the phone and greeting people, she knows exactly what to say and do."

THE SECRETS OF BRUCE'S SUCCESS

Secret 1: Know How to Sell

"I'd have to say a lot of my success is because of my background in telemarketing. I'm not a telemarketer per se now, but so much of my business involves calling people up—sometimes strangers—and making deals. In fact, my day is not complete until I close a deal. I live for the excitement.

"I can cover more ground in six hours than three people without my experience can cover in one day. Cold calls are essential to any sales business . . . and we are in a sales business. Rejection doesn't bother me for more than a second—and then I'm on to the next call. I figure the no's I get only bring me closer to a yes."

Secret 2: Protect Your Business Interests

"I've had more than one instance where I had to unleash our attorneys on someone for their unauthorized usage of our Let's Get Ready to Rumble® brand. Once, Warner Bros. paraphrased LGRTR in one of their promotional spots, so I had to get after them. A year or so later, they approached me wanting to license our brand to title a film that they had in production. After ongoing negotiations over a period of six months, they finally agreed to pay the large license fee I proposed and the film—*Ready to Rumble*—was released. I am very proud of that deal."

Secret 3: Don't Be Afraid to Fail

"Life is a learning experience. That's how I look at success and failure. In my book, there is no such thing as a stupid mistake. Unless you make it more than once. The secret to success is to try things. If they don't work out, fine. Learn from them and move on.

"I believe that you have to fail in order to succeed. And I have failed. Looking back on those failures, I can see two big mistakes I made. One was when I got involved in selling products that I had no passion for. The other was when I got involved with the wrong people.

"I have no time for dishonest people. If I'm lied to once, I walk away—because they will lie again. And nowadays, I make it a point to turn down deals unless I have both a passion for the product and a good feeling about the people I'm going to be working with.

"At this point in my life I don't need to chase after money. If it's just about that, I know the venture will be short-lived. Without passion and integrity, the business won't have what it needs to work and I won't have what I need inside me to succeed. I believe that if I help everyone around me achieve their income goals, we will all be successful. Working as a team—that's what the Buffer Enterprises, Inc. business model is all about."

Secret 4: Avoid "Ego" Advertising

"For the most part, I am in the branding business. When I look around at what many of the big advertising companies do—agencies that represent Fortune 500 companies—I am appalled at how much money is wasted.

"Generalized advertisements that are not targeted to a specific audience and that do not convey a message of benefit to that audience are wasteful and foolish.

"This is so common in radio, TV, and magazine advertising. So many of the ads you see today do nothing to promote brand awareness. They are obviously extremely expensive, yet they do nothing. They are clever sometimes. Even entertaining. But they don't make you want to buy the product.

"This kind of ego advertising takes away money—sometimes lots of money—from the bottom line. It flatters the egos of corporate big-wigs, but it does nothing to fatten the pockets of shareholders."

Secret 5: Take a "Three Strikes and You're Out"
Approach to Business Dealings

"I call this my baseball theory. I'll make three attempts to get someone to give me a response, return my call, or provide feedback. If I don't get it, it's time to pick up my chips and move on to the next table."

Secret 6: Treat Others with the Same
Respect You Wish to Be Treated With

"Learn how to deal with different types of personalities—and there are many. You need to know how to relate to all people or you won't be able to work with them."

WHAT'S NEXT FOR BRUCE?

Bruce's net worth is a solid seven figures and growing, but he's not interested in retiring any time soon. Sure, he works hard. But it's work he loves and believes in. And why shouldn't he continue announcing into his sixties? He intends to work as long as he enjoys what he's doing and remains passionate about it.

"I've made a good amount of money twice before in my life, and had a lot of fun *not* holding on to it," said Bruce. "But it's important to me to treat this third go-round—which is the most lucrative and fun one yet—as the last go-round. I want to do it right.

"My plan is to save over 50 percent of my net earned income while living life the way I want to. As far as earnings from ventures and licenses

I create from our Ready to Rumble brand, the sky is the limit . . . and I am always ready to fly.

"I have retirement accounts set up and I'm investing wisely in real estate and other diversified areas. I always keep three years' worth of cash—enough to live the lifestyle I am accustomed to in the event anything happens. (Don't be in denial about this possibility, because life can change in a millisecond.) My goal is to have more than enough for my later years and, if needed, for my loved ones, who have always been there for me."

HOW YOU CAN FOLLOW BRUCE'S PATH TO SUCCESS

- Master a financially valued skill, like sales or marketing.
- Don't let anybody stop you. Believe in yourself and your ability to fulfill your dreams and goals. No matter how big or how small, they are all important to your overall success.
- Have passion for your work. It will fuel your drive and creativity.
- Take care of your health. Get plenty of sleep, work out, eat right, and keep your mind sharp.
- Work hard, play hard, and relax whenever you can to recharge.

CHAPTER 6

JUSTIN FORD

ACHIEVING A RADICAL FINANCIAL TRANSFORMATION: HOW TO GO FROM BANKRUPTCY TO MILLIONAIRE IN SIX YEARS

When Justin Ford sat down in 2005 and tallied his net worth, he was surprised to see that his real estate holdings alone were worth more than a million dollars.

It didn't seem possible that he had acquired that much wealth in so short a time. Four years earlier, on his 40th birthday, he had spent an hour adding up his assets and debts. The net result, he shuddered to remember, had been exactly zero.

Not that he should have been embarrassed by zero. That was a considerable improvement from that very dreary February day in 1999 when he had finally given up on a bad business and a spiraling orbit of debt and declared personal bankruptcy.

Six years. What a transformation!

After working his way through college as a bartender, Justin traveled around Europe and the United States for a few years before beginning a career as a salesman for a Manhattan-based firm that bartered advertising space for a variety of products. "It was basically a telemarketing operation," he said, "but it required a little bit of financial sophistication.

"I didn't have any training or experience when I started," he said, "but I pretended I did and bluffed my way through the first several months of phone calls. Eventually, I figured it out and began to like the challenge. Within six months, I was the company's leading broker."

Justin combined a ferocious ambition to succeed with "an Irishman's natural proclivity for malarkey." Once he made it to the top of the company's pecking order, pride kept him there. "On the first of every month, my boss would print out a list of the previous month's top producers. I loved seeing my name on the top of the list. I was proud of the fact that I was outselling guys who had been there for years. For me, selling was a sport. And when I play sports, I'm very competitive."

MAKING TOUGH DECISIONS

Through hard work, long hours, and a developing skill for selling, Justin was on a fast track to a lucrative executive position. "Everything was going well. My wife and I bought a house, two new cars, and a truckload of furniture. I didn't think about budgeting or saving at the time, because my income was good and it was going to be getting better. When my wife went shopping, she usually came home with designer labels.

"The joyride came to a crashing end when I realized I could no longer do what they were asking me to do."

Part of Justin's training for the executive position he had accepted involved the valuation of the products that his business traded for television and radio time. "Basically, the company was doctoring up the retail prices of everything they were selling and doctoring down the items they were buying. They had plenty of good explanations for what they were doing, but at some level I was involved in a sham.

"I tried to rationalize it for a while and then I tried to ignore it, because the money I was making was good and the money I was promised was even better. But after a few weeks of hand wringing, my Catholic school education got the better of me. So I walked in and told my boss that he had to clean up the system or I would be leaving.

"He cut me a severance check the next day and wished me good luck in my travels. 'You're an honest guy,' he said to me as I walked out the door. 'I just hope you can stay honest and still make a living.'"

ASKING FOR—AND IGNORING—GOOD ADVICE

To keep cash coming in the door, Justin worked temporary jobs (everything from construction to door-to-door selling) while devoting his evening hours and weekends to a business he'd always wanted to develop. His idea was to get into import-export through a family connection.

He did quite a few things right. He contacted businesspeople he knew overseas who might be able to sell his products, and he lined up suppliers of liquidation-priced inventories. He sought advice from SCORE (the Service Corps of Retired Executives). His contact there ended up being Saul, a septuagenarian Israeli immigrant who'd retired from a very nice career as an importer. His key advice to Justin: specialize in selling one product to one country. Then, after you have success with that, you can branch out into some similar, related products.

Justin promptly ignored Saul's advice. He had contacts in many different industries and many different countries. He decided he'd make use of them all. He did a few deals in Europe and Latin America, but he never specialized enough in any one market or industry to develop true expertise. He had no understanding of what his clients wanted most at any given time, and he didn't bother to keep current on exactly what his competition was doing.

But Justin's biggest mistake was to trust an honest but ultimately incompetent agent in one of the countries he was exporting to. The agent identified four or five products that he said he'd have no trouble selling, and did a successful deal for Justin with one of them. Then Justin went out on a limb and bought a sizeable inventory of other products the agent said he could sell.

But it turned out the man was more optimistic than capable. The agent wasted time trying to sell a hodge-podge of products that had limited appeal, and Justin lost the bulk of what was then a very limited net worth. Worse, he ended up tens of thousands of dollars in debt. Worse still, the debt he had used to finance the inventories was credit card debt . . . which continued to grow at high interest rates.

Although Justin's foray into the import-export business was done on a shoestring, it still cost more than $20,000. And this debt came at a very bad time. He and his wife had just separated—so, suddenly,

Justin had two households to support as well as a business that was in the red. To try to get out of the hole, he worked two jobs.

"I stopped exporting. Instead, I worked for a start-up publishing company and bartended on weekends. This was keeping me busy 60 and 70 hours a week. I didn't have time to take on anything extra."

Justin struggled to make ends meet, but he couldn't keep the debt from growing. "I did my best to cut expenses when the business went bust and my wife and I separated, but my overall expenses went up because we were now two households. And my income was peanuts."

FALLING OFF THE HORSE . . . AND FINDING THE COURAGE TO CLIMB BACK ON

Justin had been promised a substantial raise when the publishing business he was working for became profitable. But because the company was undercapitalized, that never happened. "I was proud of the work we did. We created a lot of new publications and improved the old ones—with me doing much of the writing. But sales never reached the level that was needed, because there was not a sufficient investment in marketing."

The two years Justin put into trying to make the publishing company work, coming on the heels of the collapse of his entrepreneurial venture, was too much to handle. He declared personal bankruptcy in 1999.

"That was the bottom for me. I started doubting my ability to make a living. Yet, with three young children to support, I had to find a way to get back on my feet. Eventually, my wife and I got back together. That was a good thing. But though it made our financial situation more manageable, I still wasn't making anywhere near enough money."

As soon as it was clear that the publishing company wasn't going to make it, Justin began networking with friends and colleagues in the industry, putting the word out that he was looking for another opportunity.

"There were no openings that were appropriate for someone with my experience, and I didn't have the luxury to wait. So when I heard about a publishing company that sold its publications through direct mail and was looking for copywriters to write marketing materials for them, I jumped at the chance.

"I wasn't trained as a copywriter, but I had worked with copywriters and knew that some of them made a lot of money. I called one I was friendly with and asked him about the business. He told me he was working six hours a day and making six figures.

"He wasn't a particularly brilliant guy. If he could do it, I thought, so could I. After all, I had experience as a writer and as a salesman. Copywriting offered me the chance to combine both skill sets."

Justin had no intention of becoming a copywriter permanently. He saw it as a stepping stone to get back into publishing. "Plus," said Justin, "that six-figure number kept bouncing around in my head."

Justin interviewed for the job and was given a choice: he could accept a starting salary of $60,000 with gradual yearly increases . . . or he could work on a freelance basis and earn the going rate, as well as possible royalties. "The salary was very tempting, considering the financial condition I was in. But I knew that if I took it, it would be years and years before I could hit the $100,000 target I had set for myself.

"I opted for the freelance position and was given my first assignment. It took me a month to complete, and it paid something like $1,500. My wife was not impressed. But I assured her that my income would go up. I spent my evenings reading everything I could about direct mail and copywriting. And I called up everyone I knew in the publishing industry, asking for assignments."

BUILDING SKILLS, EXPERIENCE, AND INCOME

Slowly but steadily, Justin's tenacity paid off. His first assignment became a "control," meaning it beat all the other sales letters his client was using. He followed that up with a few other modest-paying but successful assignments. And he soon acquired a reputation for doing thorough research and for his willingness to rewrite a piece of promotional copy until it pulled in a profit for his client.

Before long, Justin had written a number of controls . . . which resulted in more clients and higher fees and royalties. At the end of his first year as a freelance copywriter, he had made $60,000. "At that point, I felt good about my decision to go freelance. My fees and my income were going up."

During the next year, he was able to work faster and was given more assignments. "By about month 18, I was earning, on an annualized basis, a little more than $100,000."

Justin knew that if he continued as a copywriter, his income would continue to edge upward. But as his cash flow increased, so did his ambition. "By that time, I had developed a copywriting specialty: writing promotions to acquire new subscribers for personal finance and investing publications. Most of the businesses I was freelancing for were doing well, and one in particular was growing like crazy.

"I figured if I could somehow hitch myself to that company's star, I could enjoy a quantum leap in income. So I started looking at the business from the inside out, asking myself, 'If I were the owner of this business, what would I be willing to pay someone big bucks for?' "

Justin had seen how other publishing companies had significantly increased their profitability by introducing and selling high-priced products to their subscribers. In fact, he had written several promotions for those products, and one of them had earned his client more than a million dollars.

"In addition to learning how to write compelling advertising copy, I had learned a good deal about marketing," Justin said. "I understood the profit-making potential of making back-end sales to existing subscribers. I knew how to identify a product's unique selling proposition (known in the direct-mail business as its USP), and how to leverage it to create high perceived value. I made an appointment with the publisher and pitched him on the idea of letting me help grow the business."

Instead of getting a standard writing fee, Justin suggested that he take no money up front and be compensated on a percentage basis for back-end sales made by his copy. "Since I was getting a good income for writing the acquisition pieces, I could afford to forgo a fee on the higher-priced back-end stuff."

Justin offered not only to write sales packages for the publisher's existing back-end products but also to act as a marketing consultant by coming up with ideas for new ones. "The publisher liked that a lot. It meant he didn't have to do any of the hard thinking or risk paying copywriting fees for ideas that didn't work. If my ideas worked, he'd make lots of money and would be happy to pay me a percentage. My share of his success would equate to two or three times what I could make by charging my regular copywriting fees."

FINANCIAL SECURITY—AND THEN SOME

The following year, Justin's income doubled again. Half of it came from his copywriting fees and the other half from the performance-based commissions he was getting as a marketing consultant for new back-end products. "I managed to pay off lots of old debts and get my family on secure financial footing. I could have been satisfied with that, but the old dream of having my own business came back to haunt me."

About that time, he got an idea for a product he was very excited about: a program to teach children how to save and invest money.

"Going through personal bankruptcy was a very humbling experience," Justin remembered. "I knew it was the result of some bad luck . . . but it was also because I'd developed some bad habits. I grew up in an academic family. Neither of my parents knew much about managing money.

"When I got into business and started making money, I never thought about what I was spending. My career was moving and the cash was flowing. So long as I kept working, I figured it would continue.

"After the bottom fell out, I spent a lot of time thinking about what I'd done wrong and what I'd do after I got myself back together. I promised myself I'd never get caught up in a spending whirlwind again. Instead, I'd develop a taste for saving and the knowledge to invest my savings wisely.

"I was especially interested in the profit potential of real estate, and I dedicated myself to learning more about it. First, I educated myself with courses, seminars, and books, and by talking to experienced investors. Then I began researching my local market and looking at properties. Finally, I bought my first investment property, using a little bit of my savings and the good credit of a well-heeled partner.

"From the moment I made my first property investment, my confidence soared. The sound financial habits I had established for myself began to pay off almost immediately. (And though I didn't know it then, real estate would make me a millionaire within a few years . . . and I would never have to carry a credit balance again!)

"I thought, 'Why not instill these same good habits in my children—now, before they get themselves in financial trouble as adults?' I laid down some rules for them about how much of the money they earned they could spend. And I started teaching them what I knew about investing.

"In addition to what I knew about real estate, I also had a pretty good idea of how to make money with stocks. My work with investment newsletters had taught me that the most successful financial advisors are those who follow the same rules I had learned to follow with my real estate investing: buying good companies at below-market prices while keeping an eye on the overall trend of the market.

"I thought my kids would resist my coaching, but they surprised me. They liked the idea that their bank accounts were growing. Then I created some games that made the process easy and fun for them.

"When my brother heard what I was doing, he asked me to teach him to do the same thing with his children. Then one of his friends heard about it and offered to pay me to work with his children.

"I realized there was a good opportunity here—both to develop good financial habits in children and to start a little business of my own. So I decided to formalize what I was already doing—creating a program to teach children how to grow wealthy."

Justin titled his program *Seeds of Wealth* and got to work to turn it into a business.

BECOMING AN ENTREPRENEUR FOR THE SECOND TIME IN FIVE YEARS—BUT DOING IT RIGHT THIS TIME

"From the start, I was pretty excited about the project," he said. "I was creating something that would not only help people but also give me a second stream of income."

He wrote the first draft of *Seeds of Wealth* in one week, and then ran it by friends and family for feedback. "Their comments were very helpful," he said. "They allowed me to see all the strengths and weaknesses of my program and improve it."

Justin used his copywriting experience to establish a marketing strategy for *Seeds of Wealth*, starting by identifying its USP.

"My USP was practicality," Justin said. "I designed this program to

be so simple that parents and grandparents who don't have any financial know-how can still teach their kids and grandkids good money
habits. With their supervision, the kids can get into saving and investing right away and build wealth from little bits of their allowance and
chore money.

"The result is that the children aren't spoiled 'trust-fund babies'
who are going to blow a wad of money once they get control of it.
Instead, they create their own success (with adult guidance) and end
up with a tremendous sense of accomplishment—as well as a small fortune—at a very early age. As these kids grow up, they learn the
rewards of discipline over time, and they steadily grow wiser and
wealthier with each passing year. The way it should be! And those are
habits that stick with them when they become young working adults,
and later when they begin to raise families."

Justin then wrote a sales letter for *Seeds of Wealth*, employing the
selling secrets he'd learned from two years of writing marketing copy.

"When I was done with that letter, I had everything I needed to
start my new business," Justin said. "Everything but the money."

To raise the money, he approached a successful businessman he was
friendly with and offered him a 25 percent stake in *Seeds of Wealth* in
return for a $25,000 investment. "Because of my industry contacts, I
figured I could get the project launched for about $15,000. But to give
myself a little cushion, I asked for $25,000."

The businessman loved the idea and made the investment. In addition to his capital investment, he also contributed some helpful advice
and useful marketing contacts.

Justin tested his sales copy by buying advertising space in a financial
newsletter. "I knew the demographics of their readership, since I had
written copy for them," he said. "Their subscribers were middle-aged
and wealthy—just the audience I was looking for."

The promotion worked, so Justin took out another advertisement
the following month . . . and then gradually expanded his marketing
by buying advertising space in similar financial publications.

"One of the things that helped a lot in the beginning," he said, "was
getting endorsements from the editors of those newsletters and magazines. They knew me from my years as a copywriter. Being able to get
them on the phone and pitch my program made it much easier."

Justin sent out review copies of *Seeds of Wealth* to just about everyone he knew in the financial-publishing industry, and then followed up with phone calls asking for endorsements. "You can't be shy when you are selling yourself," he said. "But knowing that my product was really good made it much easier to make those phone calls."

Despite positive initial marketing results, it took a while for *Seeds of Wealth* to start posting profits. Justin continued to work 10-hour days as a freelance copywriter and marketing consultant. Then, after the kids went to bed and on weekends, he turned his attention to marketing his dream project.

GETTING YOUR MONEY TO WORK FOR YOU

After 12 months, Justin looked over his financial statements and realized his new part-time business had taken in over $100,000. He plowed most of that back into marketing and improving the product, while he paid his living expenses out of his six-figure income as a copywriter and marketing consultant.

Justin's post-bankruptcy determination to keep his spending in check had allowed him to accumulate an investment stockpile of $30,000 by the end of his second year as a copywriter. He parlayed that into real estate, taking advantage of the strong market that existed in 2001, and made a quick profit of $85,000.

"That gave me the confidence to make additional investments in real estate," he said. "In the next four years, I invested in about a dozen properties, either as the sole owner or as a partner."

Justin's timing couldn't have been better. With property appreciating 20 and 30 percent a year, he was getting 80 and 100 percent returns on his investments (ROIs) on a yearly basis. "When prices are rising, leverage is your friend," he explained. "I was aggressive about financing those deals so I could have as much money as possible working for me while the market was rising."

He wasn't foolish enough to think that the success he was enjoying in real estate was the result of some special genius. "I knew that I was in the right place at the right time, and that sooner or later the boom would bust. But I also knew that real estate was the preferred investment of the super-rich. So I continued to force myself to learn as much as I could about it."

Justin made a deal with one of the publishers he worked with to take over the day-to-day management of *Seeds of Wealth*. That gave him time at night and on weekends to study and practice his new passion for real estate.

"*Seeds of Wealth* was giving me a nice, steady second stream of income," Justin said. "But real estate was offering me the chance to accumulate equity fast. I couldn't ignore that opportunity."

Justin's full-hearted jump into the world of real estate gave him an advantage that made a big difference. "A lot of the people I knew who were investing in real estate at the time never tried to really understand the market," he said. "They were making money even though they didn't know why. So they didn't think they needed to learn much about it.

"I understood that investing in real estate was like investing in anything else. The more you know, the fewer stupid mistakes you make . . . and the more money you make in the long run."

BECOMING AN EXPERT IN YET ANOTHER FIELD

Justin's assiduous studying paid off in two ways. First, he was able to anticipate the market slowdown in time to make adjustments to his investments. And second, he began to write about his experiences in my *Early to Rise* e-zine.

Instead of taking a straight fee for his editorial contributions, he made a deal to create a real estate investing program for *Early to Rise* and share in some of the profits. "I approached *ETR*'s management team with the same deal I had used for my financial-publishing client: 'If I can make you extra back-end money, would you be willing to let me take a percentage?' "

The practical experience Justin got from buying and selling properties on a regular basis, combined with the factual knowledge he acquired while creating *ETR*'s real estate investing program (*Main Street Millionaire*) turned Justin into a bona fide expert.

Real estate investing was a major factor in Justin's fast transition from having a net worth of zero in 2001 to being a millionaire four years later. Starting with that first $35,000 investment, he was able to create hundreds of thousands of dollars in profits every year. And some of his rental properties were also throwing off cash.

JUSTIN FORD'S THREE RULES FOR INVESTING IN REAL ESTATE

When asked for his "best advice" for investing in real estate, Justin said, "There is a lot to learn about real estate investing if you want to do it on a full-time basis. But if you stick to these three rules you won't go wrong, even if you don't spend the time I did studying the details:

"First, make sure you get a fixed-rate mortgage.

"Second, make sure your properties will cash flow. (To do that, you have to know your market thoroughly, including how much you can reasonably charge for rent.)

"Finally, make sure you *always* buy under value."

"It became more difficult to do as real estate prices rose," admitted Justin. "But in the early days I was able to buy rental properties with minimum down payments and be in a cash positive situation a year or two later."

TAKING REAL ESTATE TO THE NEXT LEVEL

By 2005, Justin had four income streams:

- A six-figure income from writing advertising copy. This was a 30- to 40-hour-a-week commitment.
- A second six-figure income as a marketing consultant. This was a 10- to 20-hour-a-week commitment.
- A mid-five-figure income from his best rental real estate properties.
- And a modest but rewarding income from *Seeds of Wealth* that rolled in steadily with almost no investment of his time.

For most people, this would have been enough. But Justin had ideas about adding a fifth stream of income to his already sufficient monthly cash flow.

Anticipating real estate deflation on the East and West Coasts, he began looking for good investment values in other parts of the country. "I wanted to stick with Sunbelt states," he said, "because I felt that in the long term they would do best, given their appeal to aging baby boomers.

"Since Florida, California, and other coastal areas had become too pricey, I began looking elsewhere in the South, and ended up in Arizona, New Mexico, and Texas.

"The values you can find in Texas today, for example, compare favorably to what I was buying in Florida five years ago."

To leverage his experience and capital, Justin is now setting up real estate limited partnerships for the purpose of investing in those still-well-priced markets.

"The advantage of creating limited partnerships is that you can get a higher rate of return than you would otherwise, and you can charge a fee for managing the property," he said. "I charge a set-up fee and a monthly management fee and my partners are happy to pay it."

Justin expects to be able to buy millions of dollars' worth of property using this approach.

"As the managing partner, I don't have to come up with much money—and yet I get the lion's share of the profits," said Justin. "So long as I buy good deals that don't go bad, my investors are very happy . . . and so am I."

AN AUTOMATIC MONEY MACHINE

When Justin was working on his *Seeds of Wealth* program, he spent months researching the principles and writing the chapters. He estimates that he sacrificed one-third of his potential income in order to create the program—but it has turned out to be so successful that it now generates income for him automatically.

The same was true of the work he did as a consultant. Rather than take fees for creating products and writing copy for them, he took percentages. "If you can cut a percentage deal rather than getting paid up front, you stand a chance of making a lot more money . . . money that keeps rolling in," he said.

His *Main Street Millionaire* real estate program for *ETR* took almost a year to complete. "I don't like to think about how many hours I put into that," Justin said. "And all without getting a penny up front." Now he's happy he spent so much time and energy on the program, because the royalty checks continue to appear in his mailbox every month.

As a marketer/copywriter with a winning track record, Justin's work is always in demand. "This allows me to have my cake and eat it, too," he said.

If a client wants Justin to create and sell a new product, he has to pay him a fee plus give him a sizeable share of the profits. "I have a high income and enough money in the bank to be selective," he said. "I'm still very good to my old clients—the companies that gave me a chance when I first began—but everybody else has to ante up if they want me."

One of Justin's longstanding principles has been to make sure his clients make as much or more money than he does. So if a promotion that he writes doesn't work, he revises it for free—over and over again, if necessary. "Companies that are willing to pay me what I want have a right to expect performance," he said.

"In the long run, your reputation is what matters. If you treat your clients well—and in my business, that means making sure they make money—you'll always be able to demand high fees and royalties."

WHAT YOU CAN LEARN FROM JUSTIN'S EXPERIENCE

At the beginning of his business career, Justin was on track to an executive position that would have given him a six-figure yearly income. Making that kind of money early in a career virtually guarantees a lifetime of affluence . . . yet a surprising number of people quit such jobs.

There is a good reason for that high attrition rate. High-paying jobs are almost always very challenging and stressful. That, of course, is why they pay so well.

Usually the challenge has to do with either performance or risk. In Justin's case, there was the added problem of being required to follow questionable business practices. "Because of how I felt about the ethics of what I was being asked to do," Justin said, "I didn't think that keeping my job was an option. But after I quit, there were times when I wondered if I shouldn't have waited until I had replaced it with another sales job that paid as well."

Hold On to Your Bad Job Until You Find a Good One

If you are lucky enough to land a high-paying job, expect it to be tough. Prepare yourself mentally for the work involved—not just longer-than-average hours, but also greater-than-average stress.

Plan to work hard in the beginning and to keep working hard as long as you are employed. Keeping a highly remunerative position requires above-average performance and endurance. You can't expect to rest on your laurels. From management's perspective, it's not about what you've given the company in the past, but what you are contributing now.

If you expect the work to be hard, you won't panic when you find out it is. If you know you will have to outperform most of your colleagues, you won't feel stressed when asked to do so.

Being happy with a job is much more about your expectations than it is about the job itself.

If, however, you do find yourself hating your job and you can't shake yourself free of the bad feeling, go ahead and quit. But don't quit until you have found another job that is better.

"Better" doesn't mean better paid. It means a job that offers you a better chance to grow and develop. In looking for a replacement job, don't worry so much about what you will get paid today. Instead, think about how much you can make two or three years from now, once you prove yourself.

And don't expect that better job to land in your lap. Well-paid positions that offer fast-track career potential are few and far between. To give yourself the best possible chance of replacing that "bad" high-paid job with a "good" one, you'll need a plan of attack. And you'll need to commit to investing approximately 500 hours in your job search.

Five hundred hours may sound like a lot of time, but it takes time to do anything well. (It may motivate you to know that most people abandon efforts to land a good job after 40 to 50 hours. Think about how much better your job search will be, since you'll be putting in 10 times that amount of time.)

Don't Start a Business You Know Nothing About

Justin failed in the import-export business for a number of reasons—lack of capital, poor product selection, and inept marketing, to name a few—but they all had something to do with the fact that he had no experience in the industry.

One of the ideas I talk about all the time in *Early to Rise* is that it is almost impossible to understand how a business really works from the outside. The important secrets—about sales and marketing, especially—have to be learned "on the job."

The safest way to enter a business and the surest way to guarantee your success is to spend a few years learning the ropes before you make the big move. That's what Justin did with *Seeds of Wealth*. Before launching the program, he had worked in both newsletter publishing and marketing—so he knew all aspects of the information-publishing industry before he created his first information product.

It's important, when selecting a company to work for, to consider not just how big or successful it is, but what kind of learning opportunities it offers new employees. Since your goal is all about acquiring "inside" knowledge, seek out sales, marketing, or product-management positions, if you have the chance. Then do everything possible to position yourself as a company superstar.

Come in early, work late, show up for training programs and volunteer for extra assignments. When your boss asks you for a favor, do it with a smile on your face. And do favors for colleagues, too.

As your network grows, ask questions. Ask questions about anything and everything. And be thankful for the answers. As a friendly, prolific question asker, you won't be held in suspicion when you get around to asking all those critical career questions—such as, "So how did you make the most sales last month, Mary Sue?"

Before you will be ready to break out on your own, expect to spend two or three years as an employee/student. (Think of yourself as a highly paid intern.) And while you are waiting, put aside your pennies. Assume that the launch of your business will take about twice the capital that your budget allows for.

Finally, keep your day job as a highly paid intern until your great business idea proves itself.

Keep Learning, Because It Will Only Make You Better

One of the keys to Justin's success was his love of learning. "Apart from the import-export experience," he said, "I've made it a point to be extremely well-informed about every business I've been in."

When he was working for the investment newsletter, he could have been content with learning as he went, acquiring bits and pieces of information along the way. "That's how most of my colleagues seemed to do it," he said. "But I was impatient.

"I read everything I could get my hands on," he explained. "I loved it when I came across a magazine article about somebody's latest idea of the best-ever investment books, because it gave me another opportunity to increase my knowledge."

Not only did he become familiar with all the major authors and books in the investment field, he began a more pragmatically oriented learning program by signing up for a Series 7 brokerage examination that required him to memorize reams of technical information. "It wasn't always the most inspiring of reading," he admitted. "But it proved to be invaluable when I had to interpret annual reports or converse with industry professionals."

When Justin decided to invest in real estate, he threw himself into those studies with the same energy. He began by reading books he found at the local bookstore, including *Real Estate Investing for Dummies* (For Dummies, 2004) and other introductory materials. He read the real estate section of the *Wall Street Journal* every day. He ordered a few home-study programs he saw on television and went to seminars that were advertised through direct mail.

"Since my interest in real estate was twofold—investing personally and also publishing my experiences—I was pretty open-minded about what I read," said Justin. "I didn't worry so much about whether it was good or not. I wanted to study the things that were selling well, so I could understand the psychology of the marketplace."

Justin's studies paid off. More than a year before the real estate market topped and then sagged at the end of 2005, he was warning his readers that it was going to happen. "If you understood the signs, it was pretty easy to foresee," he said. "I am happy to say that I got myself, a few colleagues, and lots of my readers out of the market well before it fell apart."

Find the Deal . . . the Money Will Follow

Justin's investment success—whether he's investing in a rental property or in the stock market—relies on one simple rule: you have to buy right.

In 2005, for example, he bought three properties with no money down (100 percent financing) and one property with "virtually" no money down (10 percent down, which he got back at closing).

"In all three cases," Justin said, "I was able to get these high financing ratios (and at low, fixed rates) because I found the right deal first. By 'the right deal,' I mean that I bought significantly under market value, giving me instant equity."

"Instant equity" means that if, for example, you buy a property that's worth $225,000 for $150,000, you'll have $75,000 in equity to start—even if you financed 100 percent of the $150,000 purchase price. And by buying under market, you'll be reducing your risk in two ways: (1) you'll have lower carrying costs, and (2) you'll be much more likely to sell the property at a significant profit.

Whether you're buying with zero down, 10 percent down, or 20 percent down, "buying right" means three things:

1. You're buying at a price that is at or below the average price for similar properties in the area.
2. Good things are happening in the area to support rising prices (for example, neighborhood revitalization projects, new construction, and growing popularity with buyers).
3. The income the property produces will pay for all carrying costs—and still generate a net cash flow to build up a reserve to cover maintenance and possible vacancies.

"When you have a property at contract with these three characteristics," Justin said, "it should be no problem to find the money to do the deal. If you have good credit and a steady income, you can go to a bank. Banks tend to provide the lowest rates and will often finance up to 90 percent of the purchase price on an investment property."

DON'T LET ANYTHING INTERFERE WITH YOUR GOALS

Justin admits that his interests are probably too broad. "It's best to find one thing you love and focus all your time and energy on making that succeed," he said.

Accomplishing any goal has three phases: deciding to do it, determining what specific actions are necessary and in what order, and executing those actions.

Out of every 100 people who choose to do something, the majority will drop out before they begin because they don't have an effective plan. Of those that remain, 80 percent will fail simply because they don't take action.

Another success killer is setting goals that are too low. For example, many people earn less than they could—not because of a lack of skill or hard work, but simply because fear of failure keeps them from aiming high enough.

Don't let these common obstacles get in your way. Establish formal goals and make detailed plans to achieve them. Then as you achieve each one, ratchet your ambitions up another notch. If, for example, you're earning $50,000 now, set a goal to reach $75,000 six months from now. When you hit $75,000, aim higher again for $100,000.

Before long, you'll be richer than you can possibly imagine.

WHAT DOES THE FUTURE HOLD FOR JUSTIN?

With bankruptcy far behind him, and a solid financial future stretching out before him, Justin's life is looking pretty rosy these days. He continues to invest in and write about real estate. And in 2006 as I'm writing this, he is working toward getting his real estate broker's license and opening a brokerage firm. "When I was beginning," he said, "I didn't have any money to invest so I invested what I had: my time. Nowadays, I have plenty of money for investing and anything else I want to do. So my number one priority is finding more time . . . for myself and my family. Becoming a broker should help me do that."

CHAPTER 7

KEN MORRIS*

COMING TO AMERICA AND CASHING IN ON THE AMERICAN DREAM: FROM $10,000 TO $10,000,000

When Ken Morris started out in the furniture business, he had $10,000 to his name. That was in 1983. As I write this in 2006, Ken's net worth is $10 million.

It took him 23 years to become a multimillionaire. Why, then, am I including him in a book titled *Seven Years to Seven Figures*? Because, in fact, he made his first million in a very short period of time.

Every business has its secrets. The furniture business is no exception. Ken sold antique furniture for four years in south Florida before he realized that his business had a fundamental flaw. For each piece of antique furniture, Ken could only hope to find one customer. That's because, no matter how handsome or special or expensive an antique may be, it can be in only one place. So an antique armoire could fetch a decent price—but only once.

When Ken pinpointed this fundamental flaw, he resolved to fix it. He experimented with several "not so good ideas" for several years— and then, in 1989, hit upon the one that transformed his future.

Ken's idea was to create high-quality reproductions of the best and most popular types of antiques and sell them at a fraction of the price the originals were selling for. "Antique furniture, particularly country pine antiques, was very popular back then," Ken remembered. "But when the demand increased, so did the prices. Most of my customers, I realized, weren't collectors at all. They simply liked the antique look.

"When I started offering them the same look at a fraction of the cost, they were very happy."

Ken set up a manufacturing plant near his hometown in Manchester, England. "There was lots of old wood available then, so it was easy to buy it up and use it for our reproductions," he said.

By selling reproduction armoires for $700, when the originals might have cost $7,000, Ken created a near frenzy of buying activity in the south Florida area.

"Once word got out, I didn't have to worry too much about advertising," he said. "Decorators liked what I was offering, because I could replicate whatever they wanted and deliver a custom-made product to them in less time and for less money than they could believe."

Ken went from a very small rented space to a larger space on a main drag with a warehouse in the back. "After a few months, I noticed that my customers always wanted to see what I had hidden away in the warehouse. I'd let them wander around back there, and, a surprising number of times, they ended up buying pieces they 'found.'

"I realized that the warehouse concept had a special attraction. My customers felt they were getting better pieces at better prices, simply because they were in a storage area instead of a fancy, air-conditioned store.

"I thought, 'This is something I can expand on,' " said Ken. And so he opened another, much larger store in a commercial center overlooking I-95, Florida's main highway. Ken painted the building bright yellow and put a huge sign on the side that faced the traffic. "It was essentially a billboard," he said. "But one I didn't have to pay for."

His new furniture warehouse was an instant success, and became a model that other furniture stores would eventually follow. As his business grew, his customers often peppered him with questions about how he did what he did and where he got his merchandise.

BRANCHING OUT LEADS TO . . . MORE MONEY

"Some of my customers were sort of taken by the romance of the business," he said. "And a lot of them were tourists, visiting south

Florida. They wanted to know how they could open stores like mine in their towns."

After turning down dozens of people, Ken realized he was turning away a serious second stream of income. Since his Manchester factory was now capable of producing furniture in considerable volume, he began telling people that "maybe" he could help them get into the business, after all.

"They were expecting me to create some kind of franchise," said Ken. "But I didn't want to get involved with all the legal regulations. I thought I'd do just fine by supplying them with furniture."

Ken knew these would-be store owners wouldn't be able to buy the kind and quality of furniture he could provide at such low prices. So when he helped them set up their stores, he took no compensation. Instead, he asked for a handshake deal that he would be their primary supplier.

Starting in 1989, both of Ken's businesses, retail and wholesale, expanded rapidly. By 1996, seven years after he had started, his net worth, including the value of his stores, was well in excess of a million dollars.

"It was a big improvement on the situation I was in when I came to this country," he said, smiling.

Several years ago, with product and labor costs rising in England, Ken flew to China to set up a factory there. "It took patience at first," he admitted. "You can't just go into a country like China and dictate terms. But eventually, I figured out how to work there—and it's getting better and better."

With contacts in China, Ken was able to expand his product line, adding bronze statues and all sorts of other art reproductions to his inventory. "The Chinese can pretty much replicate anything made in the West at a fraction of the cost. Once you get to know what they can do, your creative mind kicks into high gear."

In recent years, Ken has been manufacturing not just reproduction furniture and art pieces (including sculptures, oil paintings, and ceramics), but also brass fixtures, appliances, and building products. The result has been a huge increase in sales. Currently, he is spending about $2.5 million a year to produce replicas in his Chinese factory. In five years, he expects to be spending close to $5 million. And the profits from those expenditures are huge.

WHERE THE REAL WEALTH COMES FROM

Ken's current net worth is partly the result of real estate. "I didn't set out to be a real estate investor," he said. "But buying properties for my stores made more sense than renting. As my business grew, so did my real estate holdings. It wasn't intentional, but it was very profitable."

Because location is so crucial to the success of his retail stores, Ken spent lots of time scouting out and selecting the right buildings. The stores had to be the right shape—not too deep, not too narrow. They had to be on a main thoroughfare. And, now, they have to have space above them that he can develop into apartments.

Whenever Ken found an appropriate location for a store, he would take out a loan and buy the property. "Considering taxes and upkeep and all, buying was more expensive on a cash flow basis," he admitted. "But the appreciation was really good. And when you have a mortgage, increasing prices can have a very big impact on your equity."

Although prices for residential properties have dipped in Florida recently, commercial values are still very good. In Boca Raton and Delray Beach, in fact, they have continued to appreciate, which means that the majority of Ken's real estate holdings are continually edging upward.

Back in 1996, Ken refinanced a few of his stores to get a better interest rate. "I was actually a bit shocked by how much the properties were worth," he said. It was then that he realized his net worth had climbed to the seven-figure level.

NEW PROJECTS MEAN BIG PROFITS

Real estate has been so lucrative for Ken that he has given up investing in anything else. "I tried stocks and some other fancy deals," he said. "But I didn't have a knack for them. And the results were very uneven."

In 2002, Ken began building single-family "spec" houses and selling them to wealthy people in Florida. His partner, a contractor who had done a great job building Ken's current 6,000-square-foot home, impressed Ken as someone he could count on.

"We got along well, and we realized we each had resources we could bring to the partnership," said Ken. "He had great industry contacts, a good reputation, and reliable subcontractors . . . and I had access to capital and the ability to furnish these houses with what looked like millions of dollars' worth of antiques from my factory in China."

The beautiful furnishings gave the homes, which were large and well-built to begin with, a look and feel that was substantially better than their actual value. "So far, we've always managed to sell them for more than we planned," said Ken. "People seem to like them straight-away. It's been a very good little side business."

The process Ken and his partner developed was quick and efficient. The partner would build one house while Ken was furnishing another. "We made it a point to keep the momentum going. And things have been going so well, we've been kind of afraid to stop."

Using his business contacts, Ken has outfitted these mini-mansions with hardwood and marble flooring from China and state-of-the-art kitchens from England. Many of the nicest pieces are custom-designed. "We have our own little real estate niche," he said. "Nobody else in the area can deliver the house we can at the price we are charging."

Ken's typical "estate home" sells for more than a million dollars. With a 25 to 40 percent profit on each one, he and his partner have been earning "a nice little bit of extra money."

COMBINING TWO WINNING STRATEGIES

Ken's newest venture combines real estate with the furniture business. He finds a good-sized lot on a main street, and then puts up a mixed-use building: a large store on the first floor and three to six apartments above it.

"The idea is to convert the apartments into condos, sell them, and make enough to pay for all the expenses of the store," said Ken.

"A variation of that, which we've already done, is to keep the upper units as apartments, rent them out, and use the cash flow to take care of all the store expenses. That way, the store operates without the burden of rent or mortgage payments."

FIVE ELEMENTS OF KEN'S SUCCESS

- Throughout his life, Ken has used his extraordinary buying skills to purchase all sorts of luxury goods for himself at amazingly discounted prices. "I can always find something cheaper," he said. "And I'll buy anything—a watch, a car, a boat, an apartment—as long as I can make money on it." As a result of his considerable personal experience as a mega-consumer, he also understands the enormous power of selling luxury goods at bargain-basement prices. "Everyone wants a good deal," he said. "In south Florida and on the Atlantic coast (where most of my stores are), getting the best deal is almost an obsession with people."
- Ken boosts his profits by offering his customers a "better deal" if they buy more than one thing. "I carry a large number of related products," he said. "If someone walks into one of my stores aiming to buy a table or chair, I think there's a chance I can sell him a painting or a piano or a kitchen, too."
- To sell products cheaply, he is not afraid to travel overseas and set up satellite manufacturing operations. "This is something most of my competitors just won't do. But for me, it has been the best way to get an advantage."
- Ken likes to talk to people. "So many of the opportunities I've had come from customers of mine or friends or even people I bump into at bars and restaurants. I'm a pretty friendly guy. If you tell me what kind of business you are in, chances are I'll think of some way to make a connection."
- Ken likes to be a partner. "I could never run all the businesses I have if I had to do them myself," Ken admitted. "I'm not that good a businessman. All of my most successful businesses, with the exception of the first one, have been partnerships. Without my partners, I would be a much poorer man. And I'm not just talking about money."

CHAPTER 8

MONICA DAY

GETTING STARTED: HOW TO BOOST YOUR INCOME FROM $26,000 TO $134,000 IN TWO YEARS

Monica Day will be the first to tell you, she never had a very clear direction in terms of career or financial goals. Like a lot of recent college grads, she knew she wanted to do something personally rewarding . . . and she wanted to make good money, too. She also craved work that offered a lot of freedom in her day-to-day life.

After college, she bounced back and forth from positions in sales and marketing to jobs with charitable organizations for causes that moved her. Her bachelor's degree was in creative writing—and that's what she really loved to do. Not much money in that, though (or so she thought). So she kept her writing on the side, as a hobby, never thinking she'd be able to earn a living with it.

By the time she was 35, she had a second child, was putting her husband through nursing school, and was supporting her family on just $26,000 a year working for a non-profit magazine. She had filed for bankruptcy after the birth of her first child when a stint on bed-rest with no income and no cushion in the bank caught up with her. Life seemed like a perpetual cycle of going under and digging out.

But the dream of being a writer one day—and of having more freedom and independence—never left her. In fact, the older she got, the stronger her desire became to do something she loved.

The desire finally became so strong that she felt she had to do something drastic. So she quit her job and decided to see if she could make a go of freelance writing. But after six months, she'd earned only $40, her computer had crashed (and she was too broke to buy a new one)—and hope was fading fast.

HELP IN THE FORM OF A LONG-FORGOTTEN LETTER

Unable to sleep one night, trying to figure out how she could avoid throwing in the towel on her freelance career, Monica remembered a letter she'd received in the mail when she first began freelancing full-time. It was from AWAI (American Writers and Artists Inc.), inviting her to invest in a home-study program to learn direct-response copywriting. "Can you write a letter like this one?" the headline asked, "Answer 'Yes,' and you will be in big demand, earning great money, writing a few hours a day from anywhere in the world you choose to live . . . "

Monica had been tempted to respond right away, but her skepticism won over and she filed the letter in her "in-box" instead. Now, she thought about the big promise languishing in that forgotten stack of papers.

First thing the next morning, she called the number listed at the end of the letter and spoke to a company representative who told her she could get started with a $79 down payment.

"That was about as much credit as I had left on my credit card, but I did it," she said, "and the rest is history."

"I'll give it six months," she told her husband. "If I can't get something going by then, I'll go back into sales."

Armed with just this basic copywriting program, a few related books, the computers at her local library, and a tight personal deadline to succeed, Monica set out to reach a significant goal in her life. She was determined to become a six-figure copywriter—as quickly as possible.

Even with a brand-new baby at home, she managed to spend four hours a day getting her copywriting career off the ground, and another three to four hours doing side projects to make a little income until the money started to flow.

MONICA LANDS HER FIRST CLIENT

About six weeks after she started the program, and well before she felt ready, Monica began looking for clients.

"I probably should have waited until I had more experience," she said. "But my family circumstances wouldn't allow it. I knew that if I had any chance of earning a living from this in the six-month period I had given myself, I'd have to start marketing my services right away."

Less than a month after she began sending out inquiries, she landed her first job.

"I found some online job boards for freelance writers, and focused on answering the ads specifically asking for direct-response sales copy. I knew it was a long shot, since I didn't have any real experience yet—and I hadn't even finished the AWAI basic copywriting program. But I didn't have a lot of time to make this work. So I offered to work for nothing—in the industry, it's called working on 'spec.' When you work on spec, the client doesn't pay unless they use your copy. That seemed fair to me. After all, I had absolutely no track record. They were doing me a favor by giving me a chance, really."

Soon, she got a nibble. A mortgage broker invited Monica to submit some headlines and leads on spec—and said he'd pay her if he decided to mail any of the copy she wrote.

"I'll never forget when that client called me after reviewing the samples I'd sent. Remember, I was working on a computer at my local library. My cell phone rang—a big no-no in the library, of course—and when I picked up, he simply said, 'Stop writing for free. This stuff is too good.'"

The broker offered Monica $75 an hour and suggested that $3,000 per sales letter would be in the ballpark of what he was willing to pay per assignment. He also accepted two of Monica's samples to be developed into full letters.

"From that moment on," Monica said, "I knew I could make a good living as a freelance copywriter. And I was hooked. I was more determined than ever to make this the path that would finally turn around both my floundering career goals and my pitiful financial situation."

There was just one problem. She still hadn't finished the copywriting program. So she contacted AWAI and raised the white flag.

"Once my initial excitement at landing the client subsided, I realized I was in way over my head," Monica said. "Luckily, I had a lifeline. I called AWAI and told them what had happened. They were also excited—but they knew even better than I did that my chances of success were pretty low given how new I was. So they provided an introduction to one of their board members, Don Mahoney. Don, a very successful copywriter, worked with me on those first two letters—and, frankly, saved my behind. It was then that I learned the value of a mentor—and how important it is to ask for help when you need it."

A SIX-FIGURE INCOME . . . IN ONLY TWO YEARS

Monica spent part of the fee she earned on that first assignment to attend a copywriting "boot camp"—an intensive four-day experience that quickly accelerated her learning curve. Just three months after that boot camp, Monica had earned a little over $17,000 as a copywriter. By the time a year had passed, she was up to $56,000.

"I'd already more than doubled my previous salary from the magazine . . . and I could tell there was a lot more room for me to grow," she said. "Not to mention, I was living my dream. I was finally a full-time writer."

At the end of her second year, Monica's income had doubled again, and she hit her goal of earning six figures.

"If things keep going at the present rate," she said, "I could be making between $400,000 and $500,000 by 2009. That's what some of the top copywriters—people I've met personally and who have mentored me—are earning.

"Or I might decide I need to slow down a little and pay more attention to my family," she continued. "I've reached a point where I can consider quality-of-life issues, since I'm no longer worried about money every minute of every day. With all the contacts I've made and everything I've learned, I'm completely confident that I will always be able to earn a substantial income. Plus, I can have a lifestyle that includes a lot of freedom and independence . . . just like I always hoped."

Looking back, Monica said she almost can't believe how quickly it all happened.

"When you are looking forward, three or four years seems like a long time. But when you look backward, you realize that it's a very short amount of time to spend in order to increase your income by so much. I'm glad I made that decision to quit bouncing around and focus on achieving this goal. It has changed my life and improved the future of my family."

THE ROAD TO SEVEN FIGURES IN SEVEN YEARS AS A COPYWRITER

As Monica discovered, freelance copywriting is a great opportunity for anyone who loves writing or anyone who wants the freedom to make their own decisions about when, where, and how often to work.

With the Internet, you can have clients anywhere in the world. You set your own rates and hours, and you can even earn bonuses ("royalties") based on performance to further increase your income. If you want to be a millionaire in seven years or less, freelance copywriting can get you there as fast as you can churn out the copy.

Monica set her sights on six figures from day one—and it took her exactly two years to get there. Now she's got a plan to get herself to seven figures. And she's well on her way.

This isn't exactly the Tour de France—with a specific starting and ending point to the race. Monica clearly began her road to seven figures a little behind the starting line. Others who might have had a solid career and decent earnings before turning to copywriting could make it to seven figures even faster.

I suspect, though, given the level of personal debt most people in this country currently carry, Monica's dismal situation two years ago is far from unique. And the way she got herself out of debt is one of the most important lessons to be learned from her story.

As her income began to pick up, Monica made some smart choices. First, she focused on getting to what she calls "ground zero" by:

- Eliminating credit card debt: Monica made it a priority to pay down her debt. And now, she pays off the balance on her cards every single month.
- Improving her credit scores: she wanted to make sure she'd

have more options and qualify for better interest rates when the time came to buy investment property or big-ticket items (such as a car).

- Setting up a "tax" savings account: as a self-employed copywriter, Monica doesn't have an employer to withhold taxes for the IRS from her paycheck. So she needs to do it herself—to regularly set aside enough money to pay her income taxes.
- Creating a "just in case" fund: she wanted to have enough cash to cover three to six months' worth of expenses in case work slowed down a bit, a client was slow in paying, or something unexpected came up.
- Developing an investment plan: Monica wanted to save for retirement and her kids' college tuition. She also wanted a chunk of savings that would be earning passive income.

All of these objectives can be easily achieved within a few years, no matter how dire your financial picture is when you start.

But, of course, taking these five steps alone won't get you to seven figures in seven years.

IF YOU DECIDE TO BECOME A COPYWRITER, HERE'S WHAT YOU NEED TO KNOW

Setting Your Own Schedule

One of the best parts about being a copywriter is the freedom. You decide who to work for, how much you want to earn, and how fast you want to grow. You can work from anywhere, and your time is your own. But don't be confused by how idyllic it sounds. This path still involves working—very different from earning passive income through investments.

"I have this running joke with a colleague of mine, KJ, who is now my business partner," explained Monica. "When our friends at AWAI would tell new copywriters they could 'work from anywhere, any time,' we would mutter under our breath, 'They mean work from everywhere, *all* the time, don't they?'

"Of course, we both love what we're doing and are very happy with the career choice we made. But it's important that people understand they will work very hard as a freelance copywriter—especially in the first few years. It will take more courage, self-discipline, and commitment than you might think to see it through to the six-figure mark."

Self-discipline is key. Just about every successful freelance copywriter would concur: you must set up a regular schedule and stick to it. You'll discover early on that your most creative and productive writing time is probably in the morning. Then, you can tackle things like marketing, bookkeeping, research, and other routine or mundane tasks in the afternoon.

A typical schedule for Monica goes something like this:

5:00–5:30 a.m.	Wake-up time/yoga/shower
5:30–6:30	Goal planning and prep time
6:30–8:00	Get family moving and out the door
8:00–8:15	Starbucks run
8:30–10:30	Focused writing time
10:30–11:00	Break/e-mail check
11:00–1:00 p.m.	Focused writing block
1:00–2:00	Lunch at desk/reading and study time/walk the dog
2:00–4:00	Writing and/or research and client/project management
4:00–5:30	What most needs attention—flex-time according to deadlines, kids' needs, administrative needs, etc.

These days, Monica tries not to work at home in the evenings . . . but admits that it's still necessary for her to do so. So another block of time between 9:00 p.m. and 11:00 p.m. often transforms from personal time to work time. Sometimes, she spends a late night working until 7:00 p.m. Whatever it takes to get the work done.

Of course, in the early days, Monica had two preschool-age children to tend to while she was balancing work projects. Here's the schedule she often shares with parents who are trying to work at home while they have young children:

5:00–7:00 a.m.	Adult wake-up, planning, and prep time
7:00–9:00	Kid wake-up time Family planning/prep/play time
9:00–1:00 p.m.	Adult focused work time (while kids are at school, friends' houses, etc.)
1:00–3:00	Kids come home to nap or rest, depending on age Adult less-focused-but-still-able-to-work time
3:00–8:00	Dedicated family time . . . no multi-tasking! (This is when the kids get your undivided attention. When you cook and clean, they help. Eat together. Play.)
8:00	Kid bedtime/quiet reading time, depending on age
8:00–10:00	Adult personal time . . . read, relax, personal e-mail and phone calls
10:00	Adult bedtime

Some people who work at home will find it hard to stop working . . . others will find it difficult to get started. Having a solid schedule in place will ensure that you don't let your natural inclinations get in the way of finding both success and personal satisfaction.

FINDING COMPANIES THAT NEED COPYWRITERS

Do companies really need copywriters? Absolutely. Copywriters have written every word you see on websites, credit card solicitations, catalogs, classified ads, eBay listings . . . and a lot of it is terrible.

The more effective your copy is at making sales for your clients, the more valuable you are to them . . . and the more they will pay for your services.

Whether you choose to write for small, local businesses or big, national companies depends entirely on you.

Small companies may be in desperate need of a strong copywriter. . . even if they don't realize it. Start by approaching local bakeries, accounting firms, and travel agents and offering to update their existing copy

THE MANY USES OF COPYWRITING SKILLS

You can use your copywriting skills to sell anything and everything—including your ideas.

If you already own a business—any business—mastering the skill of copywriting is imperative. If you don't own a business, I would argue that mastering the skill of copywriting would be the most natural first step toward starting one.

Every single type of business depends on an exchange of money for a product or service of value. Before that exchange happens, there has to be a communication that proves the worth of what's being sold. Copywriting skills will improve that communication—and naturally earn your business more money—no matter what you do.

Monica, for example, channeled her copywriting prowess into a business. In 2005, Monica and KJ launched their own company: Prepaid Copywriting. They offer a free e-letter aimed at new copywriters, *The Copy Protégé* (www.copyprotege.com), which is helping them develop their writing styles while they create a line of information products ("how to" books and special reports, for example). Meanwhile, they're building up a subscriber list of budding copywriters that they will be able to market those products to.

or write an entirely new promotion for them. Then keep a portfolio of your best work for these small clients to show to bigger clients.

Many of the larger companies—think Rodale, Agora, Phillips, and Boardroom—have an insatiable need for copywriters. These companies produce copy by the boatload, and you could have a good chance of working for one of them after you hone your skills with smaller clients.

While some companies will be harder to breach than others, you are sure to get jobs if you are good at what you do. The bottom line is this: if your copy sells the client's product, you're going to be in demand.

Although Monica had her fair share of small, local clients early on, she set her sights on a specific top direct mailer—her dream client—and was determined to break into that company as quickly as possible.

To do so, she hit the books. She studied everything she could find about the company—its past promotions, its products, its style, its image, its typical customer. Once she felt that she knew the company inside and out, she offered to write for them on spec—and her strategy worked. She landed an assignment that led to a continuing stream of regular work.

A lot of beginners don't want to do work on spec. They are afraid it will be a problem later, when they want to charge higher fees. But as Monica quickly learned, all it takes is one success, and you'll have no trouble charging a fee and even earning royalties for subsequent assignments.

Many other newbies have done the same thing to secure work with their dream clients. While major mailers often receive overtures from beginners who aren't really ready to take on their work—a few stand out and get noticed. Many new copywriters who have taken the time to study promotions written by the best copywriters, to work with coaches or mentors, and to work hard to develop their skills find that doors open to them more readily than they might have dared hope.

PREACHING TO THE COPYWRITING-FRIENDLY CHOIR

I've often said that copywriters should stick with marketing themselves to people who already know what direct-response copywriting is, understand its value to their company, and are willing to pay for it.

Monica, however, initially did the exact opposite—with understandably poor results.

Early in her new career, she arranged for a meeting with a good friend and former employer—and sold him on the idea of infusing his old-school dairy distribution business with a few direct-response tricks: a monthly flyer with a discount offer that his sales team could distribute; a weekly e-letter to his customers that informed them about new brands they were carrying and offered a free sample of some sort with an order; and direct mail targeted to his most loyal customers that enrolled them in a referral program or a customer loyalty program aimed at increasing existing sales.

"My ideas were endless," Monica said. "And so was my friend's enthusiasm. I crafted a 12-month marketing program and was only going to charge him $500 a month to carry it out. That was quite a deal, considering he'd spent $100,000 the year before to have a car painted with his logo drive around some high-profile sports events in the city."

The problem?

"His crusty sales force, all of them veterans of more than 20 years in the business, had never heard of any of my ideas before . . . and they never wanted to hear about them again!" said Monica. "Clearly, without their buy-in, this 'newfangled' approach to boosting sales wasn't going to work."

Since being shot down, Monica sticks with clients who understand the value of what she does. And there's certainly no shortage of them.

GATHERING SAMPLES AND EXPERIENCE

No one starts out with experience in any field, but that shouldn't stop you from getting your foot in the door. A low-pressure way to get started as a copywriter is to convince a few friends to let you write something for their businesses.

Monica, for instance, appealed to a chiropractor friend who had a new practice. She helped craft his ads and launch a monthly e-letter . . . and added him to her client list. KJ had a friend who sold space ads for a phone directory. She had her friend distribute her cards whenever local businesses wanted an ad but didn't have the time or skills to write it themselves.

Another way to get your foot in the door with some top clients is by attending events geared to the direct-response industry—AWAI's annual copywriting boot camp, for example. You get a chance to meet more than a dozen direct marketers who are looking for copywriters. And many of these companies hand out spec assignments to boot camp attendees. All you have to do is follow through.

Many companies attend such events specifically to find fresh, up-and-coming copywriters. Successful and experienced copywriters are often booked for months in advance. Sometimes, getting a shot with a major mailer is as simple as being in the right place at the right time—when they need something done fast and their usual writers are booked. If you attend conferences and build a network of industry contacts, the chances that you'll know when such a window opens will improve.

This is exactly how Monica landed work with one of her big clients, Nightingale-Conant. KJ was already working for them regularly—but she was booked to the gills. When her contact asked if she knew anyone who could do a quick two-page letter, KJ referred them to Monica. She also coached Monica on that first assignment to help her get the right tone and approach. Monica has since done the same for other new writers.

USING YOUR CURRENT CAREER TO BOOST YOUR COPYWRITING CAREER

When you can layer your copywriting skills over another skill—especially in a technical field—you've got a powerful combination going that can only increase your value in the marketplace. Bob Bly, for example, was an engineer who became a copywriter—and he achieved enviable success by combining his two areas of expertise.

Another angle to consider is that you probably have contacts in your old industry. Simply call up your old boss and colleagues to let them know you've switched over to copywriting . . . and ask who's in charge of hiring creative types for the company. Connections like these can give you an edge that someone without your prior experience won't have—so you might as well put it to work for you.

Copywriting is used in a wide variety of fields: healthcare, travel, finance, technical, catalog sales, non-profit fundraising, real estate, to name just a few. Keep your eyes open for mailings—and online promotions—that are generated in your field of expertise. Put those clients on the top of your list of people to market your services to when you're ready.

ESTABLISHING YOUR FEES

Monica certainly did her fair share of work on spec—but that's only a means to an end. When the spec work turns into paying assignments, be prepared to quote your fee—and then keep edging it up as your copy produces results for your clients.

A good rule of thumb is to start by setting an hourly rate for your services. In the beginning, you can probably charge between $50 and $75 an hour. Once you've gained more experience, you can start charging $100 or more per hour. Then use your hourly rate as a guideline to establish set fees for longer or shorter jobs.

Keep in mind that many factors will affect what you can charge— your track record, what other copywriters charge, the norm for the industry or company, and the type of project you're working on, for example.

Make sure that no matter what your skill level is, you always charge a fair price . . . and that you deliver your best.

Copywriter Chris Marlow's *2005 Freelance Copywriter Fee & Compensation Survey* (www.freelancewritingsuccess.com/marlow.php) makes the "what to charge" question a little easier to answer. Using her position as a copywriting coach, as well as her many years of experience in the business, she provides a great overview of the going rate for a wide variety of projects.

DEVELOPING A NETWORK OF PEERS AND MENTORS

Monica credits much of her success to the development of a solid network of peers and mentors.

Attending that first AWAI boot camp meant such a leap forward for Monica—financially and professionally—that she has returned every year. She emphasizes that it's important to get to know not only the expert presenters who are on hand at such events, but the other new- and mid-level copywriters as well. Being able to draw on a wide variety of people for feedback helps make every assignment as good as it can be before it gets turned in to the client.

"I almost never turn something in without first turning it over to a second set of eyes, unless I'm really under the gun of a tight deadline," said Monica.

You can use a paid coach who will make a commitment to be at your disposal in exchange for a monthly or hourly fee. Or you can develop a network of copywriters you respect and take turns review-ing copy for one another.

Finding a mentor can be a bit more challenging. Monica has been fortunate to land junior copywriting assignments with some of the same clients as top copywriters, which puts her in a position to be mentored by them. Top mailers will often place up-and-coming writ-ers with seasoned pros to foster their learning and help them get up to speed as quickly as possible.

(For detailed advice on how to find a mentor, see Chapter 10.)

COPYWRITING MASTERS REVEAL HOW IT'S DONE

Monica is just one in a long line of people I know who have used copywriting as a vehicle to build wealth.

First, I'll Tell You My Story . . .

When I wrote my first promotion, I had a yearly income of $70,000. The next year, I think my income was something like $350,000. And the year after that, I earned my first million. I also remember that about two weeks after that package was put in the mail, I was watch-ing the results come in—and they were pouring in. I realized that my commissions for that one single day were going to be $7,000. I remember how ecstatic I was . . . realizing that this extra $7,000 was on top of the salary I was already earning . . . and that it was just for one day . . . and that the following day I'd earn thousands more!

I suppose I'll always remember that promotion because it was my first. And as far as reputation goes, well . . . it made me.

I was once asked whether I believe studying the winning works of successful copywriters factored into my own success as a copywriter.

Of course I do.

And if you want to become a successful copywriter, you need to do what I did. Study the work of good copywriters by reading—as sug-gested in the AWAI copywriting program—one new promotion every day. And study the best ones intensely, so you can really master the specific secrets that make them so good.

I studied master copywriters like Gene Schwartz, Jay Abraham, Pat

Garrard, Peter Betuel, Gary Bencivenga, Ted Nichols, Gary Halbert, Dick Sanders, and Bob Bly. Most of these men were my contemporaries, writing at the same time as I was.

From Peter Betuel, for example, I learned a brilliant technique for laying out magalog copy.

Magalogs are special. They are not like ordinary sales letters that go on in a linear fashion. They are read like magazines. The reader scans them up and down, down and up, back and forth. So, to give structure to the magalog, Betuel first writes the headlines on a big sheet of paper. Then he figures out how much copy he needs to devote to each headline by laying it out graphically. By doing this—boxing off the copy and attaching strong headlines to it—he is able to figure out how to emphasize what he thinks is important.

Here's another example. From Gene Schwartz, I learned how to write what he called a "fascination"—intriguing bulleted sales copy that makes the person reading it want to learn more.

While reading the promos Gene wrote for *Boardroom Reports*, I realized that bullets don't have to be dull. He found a way to make them interesting by making them very specific. I analyzed what he did and also what some other good bullet writers (like Bob Bly and Gary Bencivenga) did. I incorporated what I learned into "the 4 U's"— a copywriting technique that is now a staple of the AWAI program (and is, in fact, used by copywriting teachers all over the country).

This type of learning by observing was a big help to me throughout my career as a copywriter.

Even after becoming successful, I continued to read and study other copywriters. I always tried to read a package a day. I was never satisfied knowing just a couple of tricks. Every time I saw a piece of great copy, I'd study it. When I noticed two great packages from one copywriter, I'd study him. I had developed a few secrets of my own, but I wanted to master everyone's.

And I think this process worked. Not that I wrote more winners ("controls") than the other copywriters I admired . . . but I had very few bombs. It was unlikely that my copy would bomb, because there was so much in it that had worked for others in the past—so many "borrowed" secrets, as it were.

Moreover, my knowledge of so many different techniques and

approaches made me a much better marketer and made it easier for me to help and direct other copywriters. Once I had established this skill, I wrote less copy myself, because I could make better money letting others do most of the actual writing. That's what I've been doing now for 20 years.

Now let me tell you a little bit about some of the other people I know who can thank copywriting for a seven-figure net worth . . .

Don Mahoney

As one of the top copywriters in the world, Don has worked for dozens of major direct marketers. He has also personally mentored dozens of now-successful copywriters and helped them achieve their dreams of freedom and financial independence.

But Don wasn't always so successful. He got started as a copywriter in 1993 after closing a custom-cabinetry shop that had put him in serious debt. That first year, Don made a meager $13,000. But his income skyrocketed in a matter of a few years.

After pushing himself to become better at copywriting, Don more than tripled his income in 1994, earning $40,000 after taxes, and his income doubled again in 1995. He was making over $135,000 in 1996 and $180,000 in 1997.

In 2004, after starting a new business, he earned a whopping $450,000. And now he also has ownership interests in companies that will gross more than $10 million in 2006.

If anyone can prove that copywriting can make you a fortune, Don's your man.

One of his most famous—and profitable—techniques is to use "overwhelming evidence" in his copy. The idea is to convince the reader of the product's credibility by providing indisputable proof that it can deliver on its promise.

Bob Bly

An independent copywriter and consultant, Bob has more than 25 years of experience in business-to-business, high-tech, industrial, and direct-mail marketing. A widely published author (and regular contributor to *Early to Rise*), Bob has written over 70 books and hundreds of feature articles. He's also received millions of dollars in copywriting fees and royalties from over 100 publishers, editors, and corporate clients nationwide, earning an income from his writing of well over $600,000 a year.

Clayton Makepeace

Clayton Makepeace makes millions of dollars each year as a copywriter. In an issue of *Early to Rise*, Clayton gave advice on how to begin a career in this lucrative industry.

"Even if you believe you have no natural talent for writing," he wrote, "you can still do very well. Good copywriting sounds like natural conversation—so if you can talk, you already have all the innate knowledge needed to be a successful copywriter."

He went on to recommend the following:

1. *Purchase a good home-study program (like the one Michael Masterson developed for AWAI). Really study it. Complete all of the exercises and become fully immersed in the skill of copywriting. This is how you learn the basics of what is considered good direct-response copy—the simple techniques that move people to action.*
2. *Get a deeper understanding of the basics of direct-response marketing by reading books such as Bob Bly's* The Complete Idiot's Guide to Direct Marketing. *Learn the industry lingo and understand the nuts and bolts of the direct-marketing business. You must understand the inner workings of the business so you fully understand how your copy fits into the equation. And it doesn't hurt to speak the language.*
3. *Study the masters. Study sales copy written by pros like Gary Bencivenga, Dan Kennedy, Gary Halbert, John Carlton, and others. Sign up for and read their e-newsletters, visit and read the archives on their websites. Learn from the best.*

    And after you have done all of the above and are ready for your first assignment (and for the cash to start rolling in) . . .
4. *Pick a niche in which you have some interest and knowledge and start looking for clients. My niche has always been health and financial publications. Your niche might be business opportunities or real estate.*

    Whatever your interests, I'll bet there is a product or publication just waiting for your newfound copywriting skill to sell it.

    Narrowing your focus on a niche market will insure that you meet your goals faster. It's a huge direct-marketing world out there; don't waste your time running around trying to be everything to everyone. Write what you know.

Paul Hollingshead

Paul, a former grocery-store clerk, is an astoundingly successful professional copywriter with many controls under his belt. In fact, early in his career, he wrote a letter that generated more than $2 million in sales.

In the 10 years after writing that first hugely profitable letter, he went on to generate over $100 million for his clients.

Paul's biggest secret to writing profit-generating copy is to understand and be sincerely concerned about your prospect. "Don't sit down and 'write' a letter to some anonymous person," he advises. "Instead, think of someone you know and truly care for—someone who could truly benefit from the product you're offering—and let them in on this wonderful knowledge you have about this product that can change his or her life. If you truly care for the person you're writing to, it will come through in your copy."

John Forde

In the 12 years that he's been a copywriter, John has written multiple million-dollar controls. To become successful in this business, he points out that it helps to be a certain kind of person—one that advertising legend David Ogilvy described as "curious" and "exuberant." But even if you aren't that type of person, says John, you can learn—and master—the copywriting trade if you do five things. In John's words:

1. *Read one piece of direct mail daily. Mike Masterson, copywriting guru and "father" to dozens of incredibly successful businesses, recommends you read at least one full promo package a day. And direct mail, said David Ogilvy, is where great copywriters cut their teeth.*
2. *Become a marketing sponge. You'd think I listen to French tapes on the way to work. Confession: I listen to marketing guru Zig Ziglar. I know. That sounds sick. But you've got to soak yourself in this stuff if you hope to make it second nature.*
3. *Feed your brain morning to night. Information is food for creative*

minds. Pack your cerebellum with deep ideas and fascinating facts. Read books most people are afraid of. Clip articles, ask questions, and take notes. Nothing less will do.

4. *Write even when you can't. "A writer," says an over-quoted quote, "writes." You can't get good if you don't get practice. Often. What do you do if you don't have anything to work on? Try this: Copy. Word for word. That is, type out or handwrite another promo. When you're finished, go back and do it again. You won't believe how quickly your writing improves.*

5. *Do everything you can to get a mentor. What do Mozart, Aristotle, and GE's Jack Welch all have in common? They all had mentors. You should have one, too, if you can get one. In fact, this may be the most vital success secret on this five-part list.*

"But," you're asking, "couldn't I do just as well going it alone?" Perhaps. Plenty of people do. For instance, you can teach yourself the tricks . . . you can weather the mistakes . . . you can re-invent the wheel. But a good mentor could slash your development time and accelerate the growth of your income.

Where do you find a mentor if you don't have one already? For one thing, you could find a top-notch copywriter and offer to work for nothing. (Not me—I'm all booked up.) You could also contact the Direct Mail Association (DMA) and look for the names of members. Offer to write your first package on spec. Look for established companies that have been around for a while. Take a job on the inside, if you can get one.

To Become a Master, Study the Masters

One last recommendation: study the most-successful promotions, and you'll quickly learn how to write effective copy.

I used to advise people to simply read the direct-mail promotions that come in their mailbox—which is still good advice. But you don't always know if a package is working just because it made its way into the mail. And even if it is working, you might not know why.

That's why I also recommend that my protégés subscribe to the very best source for studying current, groundbreaking controls: AWAI's *Monthly Copywriting Genius* program. Every month, via the MCG website (www.monthlycopywritinggenius.com), you receive a

JOHN FORDE'S TOP SALES AND MARKETING BOOKS

Two of the most financially valuable skills I know of are selling and marketing. So if you're considering developing one or both of these skills in order to increase your income and start building your wealth, you'll be interested in the following list of books that I asked copywriting expert John Forde to put together. Here's John's list . . . along with his comments on each one.

1. *Scientific Advertising* by Claude Hopkins. This is the granddaddy of all "how to" books on writing advertising copy. It's a lean, easy read with very direct advice on how to write copy that sells. You can find this one free online. Just type the title into www.google.com.

2. *Ogilvy on Advertising* by David Ogilvy. No doubt about it . . . David Ogilvy was a genius. In this book, he shows you not only how to sell in print but also how to run an agency, hire writers, pitch campaigns, and more. Another very quick, easy read.

3. *Tested Advertising Methods* by John Caples. This isn't exactly the kind of book you read in a single sitting. It's so dense with tips and examples that you couldn't possibly absorb it all at once. A bit like reading an encyclopedia of what works. Essential, though, as a shelf reference.

4. *The Copywriter's Handbook* by Bob Bly. Oft recommended by yours truly, as well as by countless other copywriters. Bly, who is now a friend of mine and who has written not just one but more than 70 books, has covered every possible question a new copywriter could ask. If you read just this and the Claude Hopkins book, you'll have a jump on half the copywriters working out there today.

5. *Elements of Style* by Strunk & White. Writing advertising copy isn't necessarily about writing pretty. But it is about making the copy disappear so the message itself can shine. Strunk & White can teach you plenty about tight writing—in fact, everything you need to know.

6. *On Writing Well* by William Zinsser. That said about Strunk & White, this book helps you approach the same key lessons from a

fresh angle. It's a little dry in spots. (It's about grammar, after all.) But still a worthy read, especially for the conscientious writer who cares enough to edit his or her own stuff.

7. *On Writing* by Stephen King. Don't laugh. I know, he's Stephen King. To some, a schlockmeister. But there's no question that the guy knows how to spin a yarn. (Consider the incredible number of his books that have been spun into Hollywood blockbusters.)

8. *Influence: The Psychology of Persuasion* by Dr. Robert Cialdini. This is a perennial recommendation of mine. I'll be frank: the science of psychology scares me. It always seems like those who study human behavior are driven a little too analytical, even mad, by it. However, this book is still a brilliant portrait of what persuades and why. Every good copywriter I know has it on his or her shelf.

9. *The Tipping Point* by Malcolm Gladwell. This wasn't supposed to be a marketing book. It is just about ideas that move masses of people to suddenly change their behavior. But then, what is marketing if not an effort to move the masses? A great read in that it's interesting and entertaining as it informs.

10. *How to Win Friends and Influence People* by Dale Carnegie. This really belongs in this list of classics. And if Carnegie were around today, he might write a sequel with the words "on the Internet" tacked onto his famous title. Online marketing is all about relationships. And this book is all about how to start them.

copy of a blockbuster sales letter. These are known in the industry as "grand-slam home runs."

You also get an in-depth analysis of precisely what it is that makes the letter great. The MCG team breaks down the letter section by section. You get their critique of every element.

Plus, you get an in-depth interview with the letter's author, and learn precisely the tricks and strategies he or she used to create it. It's like "getting inside the head" of some of the greatest copywriters of our day.

By the time you're done, you have a full and clear understanding of what made the letter work so well. And you have dozens of ideas for how you can apply that understanding to your own sales letters or marketing efforts.

I can't think of a better way to become a top copywriter.

MONICA'S BRIGHT FUTURE IN COPYWRITING

What are Monica's plans to reach seven figures?

Her short-term goal is to use her copywriting to generate a fairly passive income stream that doesn't involve a fee-for-project structure.

Her long-term goal is to apply what she and KJ are learning while developing their company, Prepaid Copywriting, to a more substantial venture—using the same business model but applying it to a different niche. They intend to generate start-up capital for their new venture from their income as copywriters and through other sources.

From there, the plan is to grow the new company into a seven-figure-plus business that would generate significant revenues and profits for both Monica and KJ *and* be a viable business that they can eventually sell.

Monica may not be at seven figures yet, but she's well on her way.

What about you? Are you ready to get started on your own fast track to a seven-figure net worth?

CHAPTER 9

DAVID KELLER*

You Don't Need a Medical Degree to Make a Million Dollars

When David Keller was a young man in medical school, his future wealth seemed guaranteed. But in the past 30 years, the practice of medicine has become a great deal less profitable. Because of increased government regulations, HMO reporting requirements, malpractice insurance, and administrative obligations, the cost of running a medical practice today is astronomical. At the same time, the amount that doctors can charge for their services has been severely restricted.

The net result is that doctors work harder, endure more stress, deal with more hassles, and get paid less today than ever before.

"My colleagues and I don't like to think about what we get paid on an hourly basis," David said. "Considering the cost and time we've invested in our education, it's not an encouraging thought."

Lots of doctors today are leaving their practices to pursue more lucrative professions. "I never considered that," David said. "I love what I do. And I think it's important. For me the question wasn't 'What else can I do that pays more?' but 'How can I make more by being more effective in my work?'"

DAVID'S FIRST OPPORTUNITY
PRACTICALLY FELL IN HIS LAP

David found his answer in 1999.

One of his colleagues, a physical therapist, was talking to him about alternative medicine—a field David had been studying since he became disillusioned with the results of some of the conventional protocols he'd been taught in medical school.

"She was developing a practice in treating pelvic dysfunctions in women. Through a combination of massage and exercise, she was achieving results surgical approaches weren't. We were talking about how, in some areas of therapy, women respond differently than men do. She mentioned that her brother-in-law, a marketing consultant, was looking for a doctor to work with several of his clients. One was a manufacturer of vitamins and herbal supplements. The other was a publisher of health magazines and newsletters. I told her I'd be interested in helping out, and she put me in touch with her brother-in-law," David explained.

The consultant was impressed with David's experience and professional qualifications, and told him that he would recommend him to both of his clients.

Things were moving in the right direction. With the marketing consultant as his mentor, David started forming his own consulting company to provide services to the nutritional supplement manufacturer and the health publisher. But there was a snag.

"In the beginning, both clients were more interested in my pedigree than my ideas," David remembered. "The manufacturer had a marketing department that determined what products to sell, and both of them used professional writers and researchers. Although they were very gracious in dealing with me, I couldn't help but worry that what they most wanted from me was not my expertise and ideas but the credibility of having my professional credentials connected with their companies."

Although David was told that this was a "standard practice" in these industries, he resisted. He tried to persuade the publisher and manufacturer to let him have more responsibility. He argued that he could do the research himself (since he was already doing it) and that it would take more time for him to direct their writers than to do the writing himself.

They were skeptical. They said that in the past they had tried to work with lots of doctors who "thought they could write" but couldn't. Negotiations were slowing down.

"I was interested in having additional streams of income, but my primary motivation was to get my thoughts, theories, and discoveries out in the open. I was already presenting some of my work to the professional community, but I realized this was an opportunity to go right to the public.

"Since I believed the government and major media were responsible for the proliferation of so much bad information about health, I didn't want to wade my way through conventional channels to publicize my ideas. Also, a lot of medical schools look at alternative medicine as some kind of hocus-pocus. Yet I knew from my practice that many seemingly insoluble health problems *could* be improved with proper nutrition and exercise.

"I was captivated by the possibility that I could one day be speaking to tens of thousands or even hundreds of thousands of people. I thought many of the ideas I wanted to advocate needed to be heard."

HE HAD TO WORK A LITTLE HARDER TO CREATE A SECOND OPPORTUNITY FOR HIMSELF

David didn't want to lose this opportunity to establish his name as an alternative-health authority, but he also didn't want to have other, less-qualified people making most of the key health-related decisions for his clients. He asked his mentor for advice.

"I had already established a very good relationship with my mentor," David said. "He was impressed with my integrity, he told me. He said that he was sympathetic to the clients' positions because he knew, from his own experience, that most working doctors aren't serious researchers and don't make good professional writers. But he also pointed out that there are a few exceptions. 'If they can do it, I don't see why you can't,' he said.

"We agreed on a compromise strategy: I'd take the compensation these companies were offering me for what they wanted me to do—and I would do extra work on my own without compensation. I would assist the manufacturer's marketing group by doing research on natural-health breakthroughs, and I would contribute ideas and even articles to the newsletter on a use-it-if-you-like-it basis.

"They both said they would monitor my progress—and if I proved to them that I could be helpful contributing at this level, we would talk about additional compensation."

The strategy was slow but effective. In 2000, his first year as a consultant, David was able to pay himself $20,286 out of the new business. "That first year, my contributions to my clients were marginal and—quite honestly—not as good as I would have liked them to be. But I worked hard to understand their businesses and improve my writing skills. Gradually, we could see a difference."

David learned from every source he could find. He read books, attended seminars, and talked to experts. His primary source of good ideas, however, came from his mentor—the marketing consultant who had "discovered" him.

"He knew that I wanted to be a nationally recognized voice of alternative medicine, and he wanted to help me. I was advising him on nutrition and exercise, and he was getting great results—losing weight, gaining muscle, and getting rid of back and joint pain—so he personally believed in my message."

As David learned more, his contributions to his clients proved more valuable—and as his contributions improved so did their sales. "It was a very exciting period. I was seeing more of my ideas out there in the marketplace, and my consulting fees were going up every month."

About that time, he began consulting for insurance companies, too, teaching them how to cut costs by improving the health of the people they were insuring. He also helped them produce an informational newsletter for an employee-benefits management company.

THE MONEY STARTS ROLLING IN

In 2002, David's consulting-based compensation more than doubled. And in 2003, it doubled again.

He was happy with the way things were going. He was now able to help many more people than he could through his private practice alone. "Getting unsolicited thank-you notes from the newsletter subscribers motivated me to continue," he said. "I was working full-time in my private practice and spending my spare time researching and writing. If I didn't think the advice in the newsletter was making a difference for our readers, I wouldn't have been able to justify so many hours away from my family."

As his second income grew, David made a conscious effort to save the extra money he was making. By doing so, he was able to invest a significant amount in real estate. His first purchase was a lot adjacent to his house.

Soon afterward, he bought a larger lot in a neighboring community . . . and then another and another. Boosted by a strong, local market for real estate, these investments added value to his net worth every year. "The money I have made in real estate has been, without question, the easiest money I've made," said David. "Most of it came from undeveloped lots that cost virtually nothing to maintain and were extremely easy to manage."

Things continued to go well in 2004, and by 2005 his consulting income had ballooned to $400,000. This strong cash flow made it possible for him to launch a number of ancillary businesses.

First, he began selling informational products on the Internet. The profits benefited an organization he founded that researches and teaches natural, non-drug treatments and offers alternatives to standard medicine.

Second, he took ownership of the newsletter he was editing—which fulfilled a goal he had secretly set for himself several years earlier.

"The natural-health periodical business was growing," he explained, "but it was also becoming more competitive and—in the case of the newsletter I was connected with—less profitable. My publisher was not as happy with the sales and profits we were producing as he had been in the past. I figured that was an opportunity.

"I approached him with the idea that I would take over the publication and pay him royalties that would amount to more than what his budget was projecting the newsletter would make. He would make more, worry less, and no longer have to do the work.

"I told him that I thought I could make the newsletter more profitable by eliminating many of the big overhead expenses that he had been subject to.

"What I didn't tell him was that my mentor and I had come up with a clever strategy that would really change the numbers. The idea was to convert the publication from a paper version delivered by mail to a digital version delivered via the Internet. The savings would be substantial. But more important, we would be able to dramatically increase our ability to sell health-related products to our readers by sending them more sales letters.

"The e-mail delivery makes a big difference. When you include the cost of printing, it takes about half a dollar these days to send a simple sales letter through the mail. The cost of sending the same letter by Internet is about half a penny."

DAVID EDUCATES HIMSELF FOR SUCCESS

Before David signed the deal, his mentor sat him down and had a talk with him. "'If you are going to be successful on your own,' he told me, 'you have to become an expert in the key skills of running a business. You have to learn how information-publishing businesses are run, how they make sales, and how they make profits.'

"He said I had a big advantage over most people who might want to get into information publishing, because I was already associated with a profitable company and they were willing to let me learn from them.

"He gave me a library of books and programs to study. He also told me that the best way he knew of to achieve a major goal like mine was to make the commitment to do at least one thing every day that would move me closer to it.

"And that's exactly what I did. To find the extra time to develop myself into a successful information publisher, I got up an hour earlier every morning. Then I did one thing—studied something, practiced something, made a phone call, or wrote an e-mail—that would help me."

It was slow going at first, because the material David was studying was so different from what he was used to. "I ran into ideas about marketing that seemed counterintuitive," he said. "So I'd call my mentor and we would discuss them. He was always able to help me make the mental and emotional transitions—from doctor to marketer—that I would have otherwise balked at.

"He also supported my determination not to do what I had seen some successful health-marketing companies do—sell products by resorting to half-truths and hyperbole. 'What the public wants is better, believable answers to old problems,' he told me. 'If you give them new solid research and reasonable renewed hope, they won't need the razzle-dazzle.'"

With his mentor's help, David launched his new, Internet-based publication in 2005. By the end of the year, it was profitable.

David didn't have much money for marketing, but by placing small ads for his online newsletter and the products he was selling in a variety of health-related Internet newsletters and websites, he was able to identify about half a dozen reliable sources for new customers. Then he was able to monetize his list of newly acquired customer names by renting it out to other companies selling health and fitness products.

In launching his online newsletter, David's mentor coached him to spend the lion's share of his time, money, and creativity on making that first sale to a new subscriber. "He pointed out that many first-time entrepreneurs make the mistake of focusing on much less important things—like renting an office, setting up an accounting system, and even printing up business cards. But when starting a new business, you have to get your priorities straight. That means making sure it will become profitable before you spend a penny on it."

While his fledgling enterprises were growing, David continued to practice medicine. His clinic had been growing at a fairly steady pace over the years, but he was sure he could increase profits by applying the marketing principles he had been learning.

THE FIRST RULE OF BUSINESS: SELL FIRST. ASK QUESTIONS LATER.

A few years ago, I read about two entrepreneurs who had two very different approaches to starting a business.

(continues)

The Wrong Way to Start a Business

The first man, a real estate broker, discovered what he considered to be a very big, untapped market. At the time, many large companies had surplus space or offices they wanted to rent, but few commercial real estate agents were interested in brokering those deals. So his idea was to create a website where companies could advertise their available rentals. He introduced his website by giving away a free ad for a year. His plan was to convert those free ads into paid listings in subsequent years. (A dubious marketing strategy, in my eyes.)

But the broker's mistake was to spend far too much money up front—$10,000 to build the website—before he'd figured out how to use it to make a profitable sale!

He followed that mistake by hiring an expensive advertising firm and paying them well over $100,000 to market the site.

Six figures in the hole is no way to start a business.

A Much Smarter Approach

The other entrepreneur, a car repairman, had a very different idea for his business: selling neon accent lighting for cars that would illuminate the road at night.

With a mere $1,000 to his name, the car repairman spent about $300 to install his first two fancy light systems, with the balance—and most of his spare time—devoted to selling his idea to auto shops and hawking his wares at various events.

He spent as much time as he could traveling around, showing off his invention, and taking orders. They came slowly at first—but single sales often led to repeat customers, because his products attracted a lot of attention and word spread by mouth.

He took deposits, enough to build the systems ordered, delivered them, and then reinvested the profits in selling more systems. For months, he put nothing in his pocket, spending nothing on office space or product improvements. He just sold and sold until he knew exactly how to sell his product profitably.

After about a year of this, he had a working business. It wasn't perfect, but it was making money. Gradually, using only the cash he could spare, the car repairman began making improvements—fixing up his shop, buying some new tools, and ordering inventory.

By devoting his attention to selling first, and taking care of the other, secondary business concerns later, this entrepreneur ensured that his fledgling enterprise would not suffer the normal (and normally lethal) cash shortages most first-year businesses encounter.

Ten years later, his company was making $8 million in revenues.

Selling Is Always the First Step

Without sales, as they used to say at the Rockville Center Billiard Parlor, "you got gots."

Business plans, product revisions, and customer service programs are all very important. But for a new business, nothing is more important than sales.

It may be the single most common mistake in starting a new business—spending your precious capital on secondary considerations. What is secondary? My list would include real estate, office equipment, stationery, business cards, employees, software . . . even (sometimes) the product itself.

What is primary? I'd put it this way: the first and most important consideration of any new business is the fundamental selling proposition. Can you really sell your product/service the way you want at the price you want?

For example, say you wanted to open a steakhouse in your hometown. There are many things that you would need to do, including choosing a location, staffing, deciding on the menu, and so on. But before you spend too much money and effort on those things, you should find out—somehow or other—if people in your area want to eat steak for dinner. Doesn't that make sense?

It's amazing how much money people will throw at a new business without ever getting an answer to this simple question: Can I sell my product/service the way I want at the price I want? Find the answer, concentrate on the selling, and you'll be making money before you know it.

FOCUS ON SELLING THE SERVICE . . .
AND PROFITS WILL FOLLOW

"I could see two ways to increase income at my office," said David. "Either we could charge more for an office visit or increase the number of people we were seeing."

Over the years, trial and error had taught David that standard advertising isn't an effective way to acquire new patients. But word-of-mouth is. So he concentrated on improving the quality of service he and his staff provided—and it paid off. David's happy patients spread the word. His patient list began to swell.

Meanwhile, David came up with an idea to generate more office visits from his existing patients: providing them with an ongoing series of carefully designed, free information pamphlets.

"We would regularly give out pamphlets with information on new services and new lab tests—that kind of thing. And the more our patients learned about what was available to them, the more appointments they made," he said.

David improved the effectiveness of the pamphlets by applying techniques he had been learning from working with marketing pros— copywriters and graphic designers—in his side businesses.

"For example," David said, "I made sure that each pamphlet had an arresting headline, that it identified a specific health problem quickly, and that it provided hope and encouragement by discussing the possible solutions and the benefits that our new service would provide to patients who had that problem."

Besides stimulating more office visits per patient, the newly designed pamphlets also helped bring in new patients. "The messages were compelling. Often patients would take several brochures home with them and show them to friends and family members who could benefit from the new treatments."

David's "continuing education campaign" (as he liked to call it) increased the number of patients being treated in his clinic. But that increase was reasonably costly, since he had to hire more staff to handle the workload.

"Increasing patient visits, I realized, was not the right goal. What I needed to do was increase my profits." To do that, David adopted a two-part strategy. He would increase the number of services he could provide in a single visit . . . and also gradually increase the amount he was charging for each of those services.

"I already had the perfect vehicle for increasing the number of services I was providing per patient in the pamphlets we were distributing. I could achieve my financial objective simply by pointing out that these new tests and services could be conveniently provided the next time the patient came in for a routine visit."

To increase prices, David knew he had to increase the quality of his services even more. "My goal was always to give my patients better care than they could get anywhere else," David said. "That meant a better experience when they walked in the door, better literature to read while they waited, more attentive service from me and everyone on my staff, and—most important—more and better treatment options.

"My business idea was simple: I'd make sure each patient was a little happier when they left my office than when they arrived."

David's improvements paid off as his practice grew. "I haven't done any standard advertising in seven or eight years," David said. "Education and word-of-mouth bring in more patients than I can handle!"

In less than two years, David's new program for boosting business overwhelmed his office. He had to hire another physician to help with the overflow. "I knew it wasn't going to be easy to find a doctor who was both educated in natural medicine and also able to jump in and handle the increasing demands of the office. I was prepared for a long, hard interviewing process."

HELP FROM AN UNLIKELY SOURCE

As it turned out, the perfect person came along . . . without any effort at all on David's part. Julia,* a new physician in the area who shared David's practice philosophy, had heard great things about him. So she made an appointment and pretended to be a new patient.

"I guess she wanted to get an up-close-and-personal look at what I was doing and how we treated our patients," David said.

Halfway through the appointment, however, Julia's conscience got the best of her and she confessed to being a rival physician. "I was shocked at first—and there was a part of my brain that said 'Beware. This is your competition,'" David admitted.

"But I'd learned something very valuable about business competition from my mentor—that you can often make more progress by sharing your secrets with your colleagues.

"The idea, in a nutshell, is about mutual benefits. If I can create a business relationship with you that is good for you, you'll want to continue it. If I try to take advantage of my relationship with you, you'll discontinue it. In the long run, profitable relationships come from caring and sharing, not fighting and secrecy."

David told Julia that he was happy to have her in the neighborhood, that he would be glad to teach her everything he knew, and that—if she was interested—he would like to talk to her about the possibility of working in his practice.

Julia took him up on the invitation—and David found himself in the position of being her mentor.

One of the things he taught her was how he used informational pamphlets to increase patient revenue. "There was some risk involved, because it wasn't a sure thing at that point that she would actually join my medical team. But I had learned from my mentor that mentoring is about putting the protégé's interests first. So that's what I did. I was hopeful that if I could establish a relationship that would be good for her as well as for me, she would see the job I was offering her as the opportunity of a lifetime."

Apparently, she did. A few months into the educational process, she became a key part of David's office.

DAVID'S WORKDAY—THEN AND NOW

Before 1999, David's life was similar to that of most busy American doctors.

"I was a workaholic, but not by choice," said David.

"A typical workday lasted 10 to 12 hours. Some days, I would see 90 patients. I was exhausted all the time. I worked for five years without a single vacation.

"Some people look at a doctor's life and think of big homes and golf course memberships. They don't realize that the average doctor today is not getting rich. He's working like crazy and getting squeezed by rising costs and tight regulations.

"When your only source of income is patient visits, you tend to do more of them than you can comfortably handle. The mentality is: if I don't work, then I won't make money. So you work longer hours.

"Longer hours often mean more stress and less quality. And I didn't want my practice to become a big waiting room that processed patients like products on an assembly line."

By improving and expanding his services, David was able to bring in more money. That made it possible to hire and train a larger staff . . . which meant even better treatment for his patients.

"Now, I see a quarter of the patients I used to, and yet the office is twice as profitable," said David. "We all work hard to make sure our patients are happy with their treatments. And they are. They tell us so."

David's patients aren't the only ones who like the new and improved environment. His office climate is lighter and cheerier—all his employees love what they do and find personal fulfillment in their work.

David's workload has dropped, and so have his hours—dramatically. Whereas he used to work 10- to 12-hour days, five or six days a week, he now works only five hours a day, three days a week. On Tuesdays, he stays home to write, and on Thursdays, he has meetings with his consulting clients.

The biggest benefit, David said, is that his new schedule has given him lots more time to spend with his wife and son. "I'm home early for dinner these days, and my weekends are free. Plus, we take vacations!"

And not just one vacation a year. Several. "The truth is—and I'm almost embarrassed to say this—I'm hoping to take five vacations this year. I managed to take four last year. This year, I would like to top that."

Despite the freedom and prosperity of his new life, David is still creating new streams of income. In 2006, he started an Internet business selling informational health products like e-books and e-zines, and he is currently working on a resort spa that will offer cosmetic surgery, anti-aging therapies, and exercise programs.

"My life is pretty good right now. I make a good living helping people get healthy. And I have plenty of time for personal interests and family. It's good to know that I could retire if I wanted to. But why would I?"

WHAT YOU CAN LEARN FROM DAVID'S EXPERIENCE

You don't need a medical degree to make big money, but you do need to develop some business skills. Here's how you can follow David's path to wealth.

Redeploying Your Knowledge to Create a
Second Stream of Income

David was able to triple-dip from his medical knowledge by agreeing to consult for a business that sold natural supplements and to write for a natural-health newsletter. Think about the knowledge you have gained during the course of your business career. Some of that, surely, would be valuable to others.

The most common way to create a second income based on your existing knowledge is to promote yourself as a speaker, author, or consultant. It doesn't really matter what business you are in. If you have been practicing a useful skill for 10 or 20 years, you know something that other people want to learn.

Your goal is to become recognized as an expert in your field. Accomplishing that can be done in three phases:

1. Narrowing down your field of expertise
2. Mastering your subject
3. Promoting yourself

The narrower the field, the easier it will be for you to become a true expert. And having true expertise is the key to being successful as an author, speaker, or consultant.

It takes several thousand hours of study and practice to truly master any complicated subject. By narrowing your field of expertise, you will shorten the time it takes. David had already developed a specialty before he became a writer and publisher. He began his career as a general practitioner with a concentration on natural medicine. Later, he became particularly interested in fitness and anti-aging. The particular knowledge he had gained by focusing on these subjects gave him credibility with clients in those fields when he had the opportunity to consult and publish with them.

MASTER ANY SKILL—ALL IT TAKES IS PRACTICE

It is possible to achieve proficiency in any complicated skill. To make matters simple, let's say that, broadly speaking, there are three levels:

1. Competence
2. Mastery
3. Virtuosity

I've spent quite a bit of time thinking about this, talking to professionals in various fields, and recalling personal experiences. My conclusion is as follows:

- It takes about 1,000 hours to become competent at any worthwhile skill.
- It takes about 5,000 hours to master that skill.
- It takes between 25,000 and 35,000 hours to become a virtuoso. (And then, only if you are gifted.)

These are ballpark numbers—and if you have a really good teacher, you might be able to cut them by 20 or 30 percent—but they are surprisingly reliable. Skeptical? Let's check it out. For instance, how many hours would it take you to achieve competence in a foreign language?

Based on my experience learning French, here's a good guess:

- 300 hours to learn—cold—the 20 most common irregular verbs in three tenses
- 100 hours to learn about 50 prepositions, conjunctions, and articles
- 200 hours to get a good grasp of French grammar
- 200 hours to learn about 1,000 useful nouns
- 100 hours to memorize gender
- 50 hours to acquire passable pronunciation

What does it all add up to? 950 hours.

That would get you speaking reasonably well, but it would hardly qualify you as a French teacher. To get to that level of proficiency, you'd

(continues)

need to do a lot more work—about another 4,000 hours of it. Say you studied two hours a day and practiced for another three hours . . . and you did this for three years. You'd probably be ready to teach then, don't you think? You would have reached a level most would consider fluent.

1. Choose a Specialty

If you are thinking about developing specialized expertise, it helps to work through the narrowing-down process on paper.

Let's say you wanted to become some sort of investment expert. You would draw a box with nine compartments—three across and three down. Along the vertical axis of this grid, label each row with a different type of investment that you already know something about. For example: stocks, bonds, and precious metals. Then, along the horizontal axis of the grid, label each column with a different technique that you're familiar with for choosing investments. For example: technical analysis, fundamental analysis, and talking to industry experts to dig up inside information.

You now have nine specialties to choose from—where each column intersects with each row.

After choosing one of those specialties, you could further refine it. Let's say you decide to specialize in choosing stocks by doing fundamental analysis. You could then choose to specialize in just one type of fundamental analysis. And then, if you liked, you could narrow your specialty down even further.

The fact is, you are more likely to be successful if you become known as the world's best analyst of P/E (price-to-earnings) ratios then just another guy out there talking about investing in stocks.

Once you have established the very particular subject matter you want to focus on—and the primary technique or skill you intend to employ—the rest is just a matter of doing your homework and putting in your time.

2. Master Your Subject

Start reading everything that is relevant. Make notes. Eventually, you will come up with ideas—even theories. Turn those ideas and theories into little essays and send them to anyone in the industry who will take your mail. In the beginning, you won't get much response. But as your

---

HOW TO BECOME A WELL-KNOWN EXPERT IN YOUR FIELD

Did you know that you can make $100 an hour or more simply by specializing in a subject you already know?

If you are a doctor, you can develop a specific area of expertise and teach it to others in your field. If you are a plumber or an architect or an accountant, you can do the same.

Not every skill lends itself to this kind of opportunity. But you'd probably be surprised to discover how many lines of work can qualify. I know one guy who makes $150,000 a year teaching martial arts instructors how to do a better job with their studios. Another friend of mine makes a six-figure income helping direct marketers find inexpensive items to use as "free gifts" with their offers. A neighbor of mine teaches car salesmen how to sell more cars. And there are hundreds of former restaurateurs out there teaching fledgling restaurateurs what they know about that business.

You can work for a salary for the rest of your life and grow wealthy slowly . . . or you can become a consultant in your field, make at least as much money as you do now, and work a lot less.

If you're interested, take a look at the American Consultant's League (ACL) (www.earlytorise.com/acl/), a program developed by my friends at American Writers & Artists Inc. (AWAI). The program includes a special report that explains exactly why you need to specialize and gives you an easy-to-follow blueprint for doing so.

Becoming a freelance expert is something you can do now or later. But if you think it's something that would interest you—if you like the idea of working part-time from your home for good money—you should start the process now.

---

ideas become stronger and your mailing network becomes wider, you'll find opportunities to publish. You may even be invited to give speeches at conferences or head up seminars.

3. *Promote Yourself*

There is a lot of very good information on this subject. One book that I personally recommend is *Become a Recognized Authority in Your Field in 60 Days or Less* (Alpha, 2001) by Bob Bly, perhaps the world's leading expert in becoming a well-known, highly paid consultant.

Bob's book is chock-full of ways to sell yourself once you have become a specialist, including:

- Developing your own newsletter
- Getting articles published in trade magazines
- Getting invited to shows and seminars
- Writing and publishing books
- Taking advantage of public relations

As I said, your greatest chance of becoming a successful and well-paid consultant is by developing expertise in a specialized area. You must specialize, because nobody's going to pay a generalist $100 an hour.

You can develop top-notch expertise in some special area of your industry. You can do that, and you can learn how to sell yourself. But all that will take a little time. And that's why you need to start now—so that you can make the transition when you're ready.

If, for example, you are currently working as a graphic artist, you want to develop a specialty in some particular area of graphic design—perhaps expertise in laying out mail-order catalogs or designing a certain kind of website. Once you are confident that you know as much about your specialty as anybody in the business, you'll be able to sell yourself with confidence.

Think about your line of work:

- Who gets paid the most?
- What kinds of problems cause the most trouble?
- What kinds of opportunities result in the greatest profits?

Answering questions like these will help you choose a specialty that will get you the $100 an hour (or more—I've charged $5,000) that you want. Think about it. Then act.

FINDING A GOOD MENTOR . . . AND THEN PAYING YOUR MENTOR BACK

When David met his mentor, he was impressed by his willingness to help without any apparent compensation. "I was a little surprised by his generosity in the beginning," David said. "It was my first real foray into the world of business, and I had expected it to be populated with Gordon Gekkos.

"Here was a guy who was already—by anybody's standards—wealthy and successful. He didn't need to be working at all, and he especially didn't need to be spending time helping a guy he didn't know break into the health marketing and publishing business. Yet he spent lots of time with me and put me into all sorts of good situations.

"That's how I looked at it back then. But now I realize that he was investing his time and energy in me because he believed I had not only the ability to succeed, but also the character to reciprocate in some fashion after I succeeded.

"Actually, I can see that all the best relationships are like that: you invest your time and energy into people you care about, and later, if they are good people, they are happy to return some of their time and energy to you.

"In the case of the relationship with my mentor, the circle has been completed. I was recently able to give him an interest in a business I had started on my own. He doesn't have to contribute anything to it—though he does—and I'm happy to be able to hand him checks that he doesn't expect and feels he doesn't deserve. But, of course, he does."

UNDERSTANDING THAT COOPERATION IS USUALLY BETTER THAN COMPETITION

A related lesson that David learned from his mentor is the value of sharing and giving, rather than hoarding and taking.

"Because of him, I've always tried to cooperate with my business partners, colleagues, and vendors, even when it seemed like I had no chance of getting something in return. And when I look back on my short but successful life as a businessperson, I can see very clearly that—not in every single case, but in general—I ended up profiting in some way."

Here are a few examples of how cooperation has transformed David's life.

- One of David's patients, Nick Carson,* came to David with a medical problem. They ended up talking about Nick's public relations company . . . and are now collaborating on marketing David's next book.
- David met Charles Pierce* at an alternative-health conference. Though they are essentially competitors in the same business, the two men have chosen to help each other. For example, though he's a fitness expert himself, Charles was very interested in David's recommended exercise program. He tried it, and gave it a rave review in his own online newsletter. The mention resulted in 400 new subscribers to David's newsletter.
- Then, of course, there's the story about Julia, the new doctor David hired for his clinic. He taught her how he was making money in his practice. He gave her books to read, and let her shadow him to learn how he diagnosed and treated patients. And instead of taking all that information and starting a practice to compete with him, she became a loyal employee and colleague.

MAKING MARKETING YOUR PRIMARY BUSINESS SKILL

Even now that David has developed several very profitable streams of income, he meets with his mentor each month to discuss his sales and marketing strategies. They brainstorm about new products and discuss how David can best get his message across to his customers.

"Marketing is like medicine," said David. "There is no such thing as knowing it all. The more you learn, the more there is to learn. If you stay humble and never stop learning, your chances of being successful continue to grow."

SAVING AS MUCH AS YOU CAN

David created a multimillion-dollar net worth in less then seven years by making improvements to both his practice and his side businesses. Another huge source of income was the royalty deal he made with the natural-supplement manufacturer who was one of his first consulting clients.

That extra money might have disappeared had he not been vigilant about keeping his spending in check. He forced himself to live on the salary from his private practice and keep all the income from his consulting company and royalty deal separate.

In just over five years, David made well over a million dollars from his business ventures. About 30 percent of it went—as it always does—to Uncle Sam. About 10 percent was allocated as "fun money" for himself and his family. And about 60 percent of that extra income went to savings.

David invested his savings in real estate (mostly land), stocks (a conservative brokerage account), and cash equivalents (money management funds). "Since I have several sources of income, and more on the way, I don't have to take any chances with my 'leftover' money," he said. "If my real estate, stocks, and cash continue to appreciate at a very modest combined rate, I'll have more money by the time I'm 55 or 60 than I'll know what to do with."

David is also putting part of his savings in two stock accounts for his son—a custodial account and a college fund. He opened both accounts when he began his financial transformation and already, he says, there is enough money there to ensure his son a good education and a bright financial future.

"In 1998, I would never have believed that, by 2006, I'd be working so much less, enjoying myself so much more, and have ensured financial independence for me and my family.

"It's a very good feeling."

CHAPTER 10

BRAD SOLOMON*

EVEN ACCOUNTANTS CAN GET RICH:
HOW TO HIT $4 MILLION IN SIX YEARS

In 1998, at the age of 27, Brad Solomon risked the comfort of a salaried job and the regularity of a monthly $4,100 paycheck for the chance to run his own business. A year later, he was eking out a meager living and wondering if he hadn't made a terrible mistake. Five years after that, however, he was able to surprise his wife with an unexpected birthday present: the house by the beach she had admired when they were first married. Brad paid for most of that house in cash. It cost him $1.6 million.

This is Brad's tale—the story of how an average, working Joe developed a $4 million-plus net worth in less than seven years.

"My life changed when I met my wife," Brad said. "She was not only sexy, beautiful, and sweet, but also a great inspiration.

"I was on track to becoming a career accountant when we started dating. She knew I wasn't too thrilled with my job and convinced me I could do better. By telling me she believed in me, she boosted my confidence. She even introduced me to the man who became my mentor and helped me get started.

"He was a local businessman who was involved in several advertising and public-relations businesses. I went to work for a business he had that brokered copywriting," Brad said. "At first, I didn't even know what copywriting was.

"That business never took off for a variety of reasons, but he stuck with me while we tried several changes and eventually began a whole new company promoting public companies to potential investors.

"From my work as an accountant, I knew a little about reading balance sheets, but there was nothing in my education and experience to prepare me for what I got myself into."

BRAD'S FIRST YEAR IN BUSINESS

The investor-relations business—like most service businesses—requires the mastery of two important skills. First, you have to learn how to do what it is that your clients are going to be paying you for. And then, you have to learn how to attract, sell, and maintain profitable relationships with those clients. (More on this a little later.)

Brad's mentor gave him a leg up on learning each of these skills. Through contacts his mentor had with the financial publishing industry, Brad was introduced to someone who was already doing exactly what Brad intended to be doing.

"He had so much business he couldn't keep up with it," Brad explained. "He was happy to subcontract some of the more mundane aspects of his work to me."

Most of Brad's initial business came through this client. Brad provided marketing services—research, copywriting, and graphic design—to him. The client then marked up Brad's bill and passed it on to his client.

"I had no idea what to charge back then," Brad admitted. "My mentor advised me to start low and gradually increase my prices as I got better at what I was doing."

That was the strategy Brad used—and, at first, it meant that he was working for practically nothing. "When I left accounting, I was making $49,000 a year," Brad said. "That first year in business on my own, I made less than that. I can't remember how much less, but I can tell you that my wife used to tease me that I was 'going in the wrong direction.'"

As Brad's skills improved, he started to raise his prices. "I was kicking them up by $100 or $200 a job," he said. "And my client never objected."

That probably should have tipped Brad off to what was happening . . . but he didn't discover the truth until his client accidentally e-mailed him a copy of *his* client's invoice.

"He was taking my bills and doubling or tripling them," Brad said. "And all that time I thought he was marking them up by only 10 or 15 percent."

THE BEGINNINGS OF A STRONG SUPPORT NETWORK

Brad realized how much money there could be in dealing directly with end users, so he began studying the investor-relations industry more closely. "I read the literature. I asked questions. I searched the Internet. But it wasn't until I took my mentor's advice and began making industry contacts that things started moving."

Encouraged by his mentor, Brad began showing up at industry conventions and trade shows. "My primary goal was simply to shake hands and collect business cards," he said. "I remember reading something in Michael Masterson's *Early to Rise* e-zine about how, if you aimed for one good, new contact a week, by the end of the year you'd have at least 10 or 20 well-connected people in your Rolodex who could help your business grow."

Brad's tendency to stay in his office and work by himself (a habit he'd developed as an accountant) gradually disappeared as he went out into the world and began building a support network.

"A part of my personality emerged that I didn't know existed," he said. "I found that, contrary to what you might have guessed if you'd known me back then, I enjoyed socializing. Getting to know new names and faces became the most enjoyable part of my business."

A GRADUAL INCREASE IN SKILLS, CLIENTS . . . AND PROFITS

At the third trade show Brad attended, he picked up his first "real" client. "I got him by offering to do an initial campaign for him on

THE POWER OF A SINGLE CONTACT

Four years ago, I introduced myself to a man with a reputation for knowing local real estate. I mentioned that I'd be interested in working with him if he ever needed an investor. He had plenty of other investors already, so he didn't immediately say yes to my offer. But he didn't say no, either. I kept in touch with him and, two years later, he called me. We entered into a deal in a neighboring town and bought and sold two properties in less than six months for a tidy profit.

That's just one example of the advantages of developing a strong support network.

The idea is to develop a Rolodex of contacts—people you can go to for help. I'm talking about people who have things you lack (like money, power, contacts, specific knowledge). When you need what they have, they'll only be a phone call (or an e-mail) away.

Start building your support network today by adding "Meet one new person" to your weekly "to-do" list. Make it a goal to make contact with someone new for 50 weeks out of the coming year. You can do so with a personal note, by phone, by e-mail, or in person. Say something nice. Communicate genuine respect and admiration and solicit some sort of feedback. In some cases, making a contact will be a one-step process. In other cases, you'll have to develop the relationship over time.

Fifty attempts should produce 10 to 20 new people you can add to your network. Who knows where those contacts will lead you?

spec," he said. "I told him that if he wasn't satisfied with the results, he didn't have to pay me anything."

Brad's investor–relations campaign for that client was a success. "That was the first check I ever received directly from a client," Brad said. "And it felt pretty good.

"It wasn't a ton of money, because I gave him a really good price. And I remember worrying that I'd have to give it back because I had guaranteed results. But at the end of the day, everything worked out fine. The publicity resulted in tens of thousands of dollars' worth of new investments in his company. He thanked me for the work I'd done and asked me if I could do more."

Brad agreed to do more, but he also raised his rates. "I didn't gouge him," Brad said. "I just raised the price by 5 or 6 percent. It was still less than he'd pay someone else to do the same kind of work, but it meant my profitability was going up."

Brad's first client also turned him on to a new public company. Based on the success of his first campaign, he was easily able to secure a contract with them.

"During that initial period," Brad said, "I focused on two things and two things only. First was finding new prospects and pitching myself to them. Second was making sure the service I was selling was top-notch."

By making sure his clients got more than they paid for, he developed a reputation for good service and reliability. That, in turn, created a steady stream of word-of-mouth new clients. And by filling up all his spare time with efforts to expand his network of contacts and promote his business, Brad was able to develop a client base much faster than word-of-mouth alone would have allowed.

After a year, Brad's new business was billing clients $10,000 to $20,000 per month. By 2002, he was ready to hire his first employee.

"Another great lesson I learned from *Early to Rise* is to take the time to find exceptional employees," Brad said. He remembered an article in *ETR* about finding a superstar who can ultimately take over your business responsibilities. When he met Tom Walsh,* he knew the young man had that potential.

"Tom was working part-time with another company in my office building," Brad said. "He had just graduated from college and was looking for more to do. So I gave him some part-time jobs. But instead of just giving him clerical tasks, I also gave him a crash course in finding and retaining new clients for my business."

In a few months, Brad was able to teach Tom what had taken him three years to figure out on his own. Now, four years later, Tom runs Brad's day-to-day business operations and is in charge of the rest of the employees.

"By the end of year three," Brad said, "we were a solid little company. We had good, loyal clients, some capable freelancers working for us, and a few excellent employees. We had pretty well mastered the art of delivering good research, copywriting, and graphic design services, but the investor-relations industry was getting bigger and so the competition for clients became tougher.

"Sure, we were going to gradually build our client base and maintain a respectable level of profitability," he said. "But it wasn't going to make me rich any time soon. I could see that pretty clearly."

USING DIRECT MARKETING TO STIMULATE BUSINESS GROWTH

Once again, Brad turned to his mentor for advice, who suggested that direct marketing might be the way to go.

Brad used his recently developed phone skills to get lunch appointments with about half a dozen powerful people in the direct-marketing industry. "I wanted to see what I could do to boost my business," he said. "I figured, why try to figure it out myself if I could get the answers I needed just by asking a few experts?"

Brad's networking efforts paid off. In less than 60 days, he had a free "master's degree" education in direct marketing.

"The most important thing I learned—and the thing that turned my business around," he said, "is the amazing power of using direct marketing with your own house file (your list of clients and other people who have shown an interest in your services). Once you've built a sizeable file that's working, it's easy to grow your business."

To generate a substantial house file, Brad needed something to attract potential clients. "I realized that direct mail and e-mail were the perfect media to reach my prospects. I figured that if I sent out some kind of letter offering something valuable for free, I'd hook their interest. The question was, what should I give them?"

Based on input from his support network, Brad decided to publish an investment newsletter. "Stock and insurance brokers have been using newsletters as a vehicle to get new clients for years. If they could do it, why couldn't I?"

Since he didn't know anything about the newsletter-publishing business, he made an appointment with someone who did: a consultant to America's largest investment newsletter publisher. "I called him up and told him that I was impressed by his company and asked him if he could give me 15 minutes of his time."

To Brad's surprise, the consultant invited him to come by the next day. "He was amazingly open with me. He explained how the investment-newsletter business works, and then warned me about five or six 'big mistakes' most novices make.

"I was very grateful for his help, and told him that, frankly, I was surprised at how generous he was with his knowledge. 'Well,' he said, 'I'm not worried that you are going to steal any business from my clients—and if you do really well, maybe you'll hire me to work for you one day.'"

Before Brad left, the consultant made a final suggestion. He recommended a home-study program in Internet publishing that he believed Brad could benefit from. Brad bought it the next day and got to work on it immediately. "With what I learned from that interview and from the Internet publishing course, I was set," he said.

At first, he could afford to spend only about a thousand dollars to market his fledgling newsletter to potential clients. But gradually, by giving away some subscriptions and selling others (a technique he learned in the home-study program), he was able to increase both the amount of marketing he was doing and the newsletter's revenue base.

About six months into publishing, Brad realized that his newsletter wasn't nearly as good as it could be. Since he had built his business on the promise of high-quality service, he knew he couldn't continue to deliver mediocre editorial to his subscribers.

Brad fired his editor and hired someone with more experience. "It's amazing what a difference a single person can make," he said. "Almost as soon as the new writer came aboard everything picked up. The renewal rates went up noticeably and our marketing response rates improved because our copywriters had better material to work with."

One day, Brad brought his entire team together—including his newsletter editor and copywriters—and they brainstormed for 10 hours straight. The end result was three new direct-mail promotions that could be used both in the mail and on the Internet. Within three weeks, they had mailed them all.

All three of those promotions were successful. In fact, even the weakest of them doubled the best response rate they'd had so far. "Before then, I didn't understand the importance of brainstorming with a small group of highly motivated, highly intelligent people," Brad said. "It taught me—once and forever—that when it comes to marketing, several heads are usually better than one."

With his newsletter going strong and continuing to attract new clients, Brad had time to concentrate on another important aspect of his business: customer service.

FOCUSING ON CUSTOMER SATISFACTION

"Customer service is the most important part of my business," Brad said without hesitation. "When you are charging a client $250,000 to $500,000 for a public-relations campaign, you have to make sure that everything you do for them is picture perfect.

"I learned the hard way that mistakes can kill you," Brad said. "I once brought on a client who had the potential to offer us considerable repeat business. He wanted to get the word out on his company within a short timeframe. I told him I'd have no problem getting the job done. But I got caught up with other problems—and when the deadline arrived and he called . . . we had nothing to show him.

"Needless to say, he was not happy. We finally got his promotion out in the mail, but it was almost two weeks late. I will always wonder how much business I lost by missing that deadline," Brad said. "He never called me back and I'm sure he never will."

Because of that memorable failure to meet a deadline, Brad now makes meeting deadlines his company's top priority. Plus, he tries to speak with each client, personally, as soon as they call. If he's unavailable, he does everything in his power to get back to them within a few hours.

"Remember," he said, "in any service business, you're working on their timetable, not yours."

The way Brad interacts with his clients is a key factor in his success. "I'm not an assertive guy," Brad said. "But I've developed the skill of being personable and easy to talk to."

Being easy to talk to—and easy to reach—makes doing business with Brad very attractive to his clients. His focus on keeping the client happy and satisfied is also Brad's trademark sales approach. "I know it's a cliché," Brad said, "but I believe you have to under-promise and over-deliver. By doing that, I know I can count on repeat business . . . and strong referrals."

In fact, the vast majority of his business is still based on referrals and repeat business. "If the client is happy, he'll come back . . . and often bring along another client or two."

CREATING A SECOND STREAM OF INCOME

In 2003, bolstered by the success of his first business, Brad began thinking about how he could start a second company to create a second stream of income and a second base of equity.

"I was working fewer hours than when I'd started out," he said, "but it was still necessary to put in 40 or 50 hours a week at the office. I recognized that if I was going to get a second company started, I couldn't do it by myself . . . I needed a partner."

That partner materialized in the form of his cousin, Will Lawton.*

Will had worked for a large healthcare temp agency and then became a minority partner in a small one. He helped grow that business five-fold over four years. He even started a small division within the company, contracting out specialized healthcare workers. He saw the opportunity for growth in that area, but his majority partners did not agree and refused to allocate time and assets to expand the division.

"During a family visit," Brad remembered, "we talked about Will's dilemma. He was generating sales—much the same way as I was generating sales. And his repeat business was growing rapidly. But without the support of his partners, he was facing a dead end.

"I remembered reading a few *ETR* articles that mentioned how the aging of the baby boomers would provide tremendous opportunities for the right businesses. Looked to me like this was one of those opportunities."

The deal Brad struck with his cousin was that he would provide the start-up capital and Will would run the company. So Brad bought out the small division, kept the division's two best employees, and set up a new temp agency for specialized healthcare workers.

Will's instincts and experience paid off. He picked the perfect healthcare service to invest in—one that was growing quickly and didn't have nearly enough agencies to handle the demand.

The new company exploded. Within a single year, its gross billings grew from $40,000 per week to $130,000 per week. The business was making $500,000 a year with no end in sight.

By 2004, Brad was making $400,000 in his role as president of his investor-relations company and another $250,000 as a silent partner in his cousin's healthcare business.

BUILDING A PORTFOLIO OF ASSETS

Brad bought his first house in 2001, a 2,500-square-foot, three-bedroom ranch-style home on a good street in a developing section of town. "I bought it for $305,000, and that was a stretch for us," he said. "But my equity in it started mounting almost as soon as I took possession.

"As far as real estate is concerned," Brad said, "I was definitely in the right place at the right time. In three years, that property appreciated 123 percent to a value of about $680,000. That gave my net worth a positive boost of $450,000."

At the same time as his home was appreciating, Brad was saving a chunk of his income every month and investing it in stocks.

"Invest in what you know," said Brad. "I learned that from *Early to Rise. ETR* applies that strategy not only to investing in stocks but also to investing in real estate and businesses. I used it to pick some pretty good speculative stocks. I wouldn't advise other people to invest in speculative stocks—but it worked for me because, with my accounting background and my years of interactions with many small public companies, it was what I knew."

The "invest in what you know" strategy paid off for Brad. During the five-year period from 2001 to 2006, his stock portfolio increased in value from $100,000 to $900,000.

"I was lucky to get in on a bull market in small-cap stocks," Brad said. "Then, as my portfolio grew, I started putting large amounts in conservative investments such as Fortune 100 companies and bonds. I also started to keep a sizeable hunk of cash in a money market account so I can access it easily when a promising business or investment opportunity comes my way."

Brad started small, and continued to reinvest his stock market profits. "That taught me how valuable a tool compounding can be in building wealth," he said. "If I had taken out my profits and spent them, my portfolio would not have been anywhere near as successful."

$2 MILLION RICHER . . . WITHOUT DOING A THING

In 2005, Brad's cousin came to him with good news. A large temp agency had made an offer to buy them out. "I wouldn't have considered selling our company," Brad said, "because I figured my cousin would want to run it until he was ready to retire. But he was really interested in the idea of realizing the value of what we'd built together, socking that away safely, and then working for the new company as an executive.

"My cousin's plan worked out fine for me. I got to make a very big deposit in my bank account, which I used—along with the $450,000 in equity I got by selling our first house—as a huge down payment on my wife's dream house.

"Everything seemed to come together at the same time," Brad said. "First the windfall from selling a business that I never had to work very hard on. Then discovering that my starter house had shot up 123 percent in only 36 months. And, finally, being able to buy my wife her dream house—something she deserved for believing in me even in the lean years.

"I had a sense that the equity in my cousin's healthcare business and in my home were mounting pretty quickly," he said. "But I had no idea that in only three years I would be $2 million richer . . . without doing anything."

Nowadays, Brad is expanding his public-relations company by employing his company's writing and marketing talents to sell financial newsletters. "It's not as lucrative as investor relations, right now," Brad said. "But in the long run it will give my business stability and a good base for even more growth."

LOOKING BACK

"In retrospect," Brad said, "I can honestly say that I did lots of things right and a few things wrong. I think leaving my job and starting my own business was the right decision. And I'm also glad that I focused on marketing and providing quality service in those first two critical years.

"I took a risk in starting a second company while my first one was so new," he added, "but that risk was limited because I knew how good my cousin was and I knew I could rely on him to make the business work.

"Overall, I think I made good choices in the people I surrounded myself with—my wife, of course, and my mentor, my key employees, and my clients. I also think I was right to keep improving every aspect of my businesses, from customer service to editorial to marketing. And I feel I was smart to build and work with a support network.

"The only thing I regret is that I didn't take full advantage of the help my mentor was offering me. I had one of the best mentors out there," he said. "But I hated going to him for help."

Brad said his reluctance was caused by a mixture of pride and respect. "I was afraid of criticism and afraid he would think I was a pest," he said. "Most of all, I wanted to be his equal. And when you want to be as good as someone you respect, you're afraid to ask questions for fear of seeming ignorant. And you're scared stiff of failing, because then your faults will be obvious.

"I realize now that was a mistake. If you have a mentor who's willing and able to give advice, don't be afraid to use him. He probably wants to help even more than you think."

LOOKING TO THE FUTURE

Brad challenged himself from the beginning by setting short-, medium-, and long-term goals for himself—something he learned to do as a longtime reader of *ETR*.

"My first short-term goal, after quitting my job as an accountant, was to simply be able to pay my bills for the first year without borrowing. That was pretty tough. My next short-term goal was to get the public-relations company to a break-even point. When I blew through that goal the following year, I felt good—but I sure didn't expect what happened with my medium-term goal. I was hoping to become a millionaire by age 35—but instead of $1 million, I hit the $4 million mark."

How does Brad feel about his ambitious, long-term goal of retiring with a net worth of $15 million before his 50th birthday?

"Unless something surprisingly bad happens," he said, "it's pretty much a done deal. If my net worth increases by only 10 percent each year from now until I'm 49, I'll be worth $15.2 million. My plan is to do better than that by staying in business and investing in real estate.

"If I can get an overall return on investment (ROI) of 15 percent a year on my assets, I should hit the $15 million mark by the time I'm 45 years old. If I hit it by then, it will be nice to know that I can retire—even though I know I won't want to."

HOW TO REPLICATE BRAD'S SUCCESS

Brad's extraordinary accomplishment—developing a $4 million net worth in less than seven years—was the result of six smart moves:

- Identifying a business sector—the service industry—that he could excel in
- Finding a powerful mentor and following his advice
- Proving himself to be hardworking, diligent, and loyal
- Using his social skills to develop a network of successful, well-connected contacts
- Taking advantage of the power of partnership
- Developing a second (and then a third) stream of income

CHOOSING THE BUSINESS SECTOR
THAT'S BEST FOR YOU

When Brad decided to go into business on his own, he took some time to think about his strengths and his weaknesses.

"I was always pretty good in math," he said. "So it was natural that I would drift into the business of accounting. It didn't take me long to realize that you can only make so much crunching numbers for other people. In the accounting industry, the big money is made by the company owners and the rainmakers—the salespeople who go out into the market and find the major clients.

"When I had the chance to get into financial PR, I realized that, though it was primarily a service business, it wasn't any different. If I expected to make more money than I was making as an accountant, I had to learn to either run a profitable business or bring in the big clients."

In fact, Brad learned to do both. As the sole employee in his business at the beginning, it was up to him to work directly with the clients he acquired through his contacts and to develop new clients by making sales calls.

"At first, I was petrified to even pick up the phone and make an appointment. But my mentor assured me that if I kept at it, I'd be fine. 'Just be yourself,' he told me. 'I like you, so why shouldn't they?'"

His mentor's confidence in him gave Brad the courage he needed to make those crucial initial sales calls. His natural honesty and charm convinced his clients that in Brad they would have a service provider who would give them fair prices and good value.

In deciding what business to go into, it's a good idea to match your natural talents and personality with the qualities that are usually required for success in the industry you choose.

For example, if you are good-natured, reliable, and diligent (as Brad is), you have the essential qualities to be successful in the service sector. If you are weak on details but strong on the big picture (like me), you might want to consider some sort of manufacturing or production business (where you can employ detail-oriented people to follow your lead). If you have a knack for expressing yourself but are inalterably shy, think about a career as a copywriter, creative consultant, or graphic designer in the direct-marketing business (where you never have to meet your clients face to face).

If you're not sure what kind of businessperson you would be, here's a quick little test you can take.

On a scale of 1 to 5 (1 being "not at all true" and 5 being "very true"), indicate how strongly you would rate yourself in each of the following categories:

- The Self-Starter: I am good at starting things. When given the chance to begin a new project, I am confident I can figure out how to do it.
- The Super-Salesperson: I am a natural salesperson. No matter what I want, I usually find a way to talk someone into giving it to me.
- The Agressor: I am not shy. I don't have trouble introducing myself to anyone—man, woman, old man, young man, rich woman, poor woman . . . whoever.
- The Big Thinker: I am a big-picture person. In most situations, I can quickly grasp the main points and the significant opportunity.

I am usually the one to come up with the breakthrough ideas, no matter what the subject.

- The Small Thinker: I am very good at details. If you want to know about a meeting that I participated in three months ago, no problem. I can tell you. I can also tell you, to within a single dollar, how much money I made and spent last month.
- The Smarty Pants: I am highly intelligent. I can usually understand difficult issues very quickly. I am very good at analyzing and resolving complicated problems.
- The Charmer: I am a socially adept person. Most people like me immediately and like me more the better they know me. I haven't met a person I couldn't make smile.
- The Wily Coyote: I am very good at getting things done behind the scenes. I'm not comfortable making a fuss, because I recognize that a big ego creates big enemies. I'm much more comfortable accomplishing my goals with a series of small, subtle moves.
- The Connector: I have loads of friends and business associates. Take me to a party in a brand-new neighborhood and by the time I leave I'll be on a first-name basis with half the people there. When I want something done, I usually know the right person to call and his or her phone number.
- The Pusher: When it comes to accomplishing goals, I am impatient. If someone tells me that he will have a memo on my desk at 8:30 a.m., I'll be on the phone by 8:40 if it's not there.
- The Organizer: I like things to run smoothly. Chaos disturbs me. When I am involved in a project of any sort—business, social, or personal—my first impulse is to figure out exactly what needs to be done and then communicate my plan to everyone involved. My desk is never cluttered. My calendar is always blocked out at least a few weeks in advance.
- The Artiste: I consider myself a creative person. I'm bored by the conventional, excited by the new and different. I like music, art, architecture—almost any subject, so long as there is a creative component to it.

In which of the above categories did you give yourself a score of 4 or better? We will consider these to be your dominant functional traits as a businessperson.

Now match your dominant traits with at least one of the businesses listed below:

- Service Business Owner: Desirable traits would include *self-starter, super-salesperson, connector, pusher,* and *charmer*. Dominant traits that might prove troublesome would include *smarty pants, wily coyote, big thinker,* and *artiste*.
- Freelance Consultant: Desirable traits would include *self-starter, smarty pants, big thinker,* and *artiste*. Dominant traits that might prove troublesome would include *pusher, charmer,* and *super-salesperson*.
- Manufacturing Entrepreneur: Desirable traits would include *self-starter, organizer, big thinker, connector,* and *pusher*. Dominant traits that might prove troublesome would include *aggressor, artiste, charmer,* and *wily coyote*.
- Information Publishing Magnate: Desirable traits would include *self-starter, big thinker, aggressor, organizer,* and *connector*. Dominant traits that might prove troublesome would include *small thinker, artiste,* and *smarty pants*.
- Internet Marketer: Desirable traits would include *self-starter, big thinker, aggressor, wily coyote, artiste,* and *pusher*. Dominant traits that might prove troublesome would include *organizer, smarty pants,* and *super-salesperson*.
- Freelance Copywriter and/or Graphic Designer: Desirable traits would include *self-starter, aggressor, smarty pants, connector,* and *super-salesperson*. Dominant traits that might prove troublesome would include *charmer, big thinker, artiste,* and *wily coyote*.

You might be puzzled by some of these pairings. Why, for example, am I suggesting that being an *artiste* or a *big thinker* might be "troublesome" for a freelance copywriter or graphic designer? Because being a freelance anything means you have to constantly subjugate your creative vision to your client's ideas. Unless you can learn to tailor your work to your client's wants and needs, you won't be very effective in your chosen profession.

Note that for almost any business career, it helps to be a self-starter. The reason for this is too obvious to mention. What's important to recognize is that this seemingly innate quality can be learned. All it

THE FOUR BASIC BUSINESS CATEGORIES

Whatever you intend to do for a living—whether it's selling stocks or painting landscapes—it's a business. And all businesses fall into one of four categories:

Retail
Service
Wholesale
Manufacturing

Retail

Retail is the first thing most people think of when they think of business. It seems to be an easy and enjoyable way to make a living—and for that reason, it is very attractive. But the reality of owning a business in the retail sector is very different.

- Usually, retail ties you to a specific location and doesn't allow for a great deal of flexibility in terms of hours or travel.
- Retail is heavily dependent on location. If your city starts doing road construction outside your store, you could go bankrupt before they finish. You're chained to your location—but still have to pay rent, utilities, and employee expenses while you wait.
- It's tough to get rich with retail. The only retailers who are super-rich have many, many retail operations. But they are not retailers themselves; they are marketers of retail operations. There is a big difference.

The Service Industry

Service businesses include everything from blue-collar hole-digging to middle-level technical work to white-collar executive work and, finally, the professions.

Yes, doctors, lawyers, and accountants are service providers. So are speechwriters and most entertainers. All share the essential characteristics of the service sector:

(continues)

- How much you can make depends on the kind of service you provide. But whether you're a brain surgeon or a landscaper, at the end of the day, you are charging for your time.
- If you want to make more money, there are only two ways to do it: charge more per hour or work more hours. And there are only so many hours you can work and still have a life.

On the plus side, the world is always in short supply of good service people. That's why the service industry is a great entry-level business opportunity. If you make up your mind to do a great (not just good) job at a fair or cheaper-than-average rate, meet your deadlines, and keep your promises to your clients, you'll find yourself climbing to the top of the ladder in no time flat.

The problem with the service industry is related to its advantage. It's so easy to get into that you will have lots of competition as your business grows. That means you'll be squeezed on price, making it tougher to turn a profit.

Wholesale

Wholesale is a pretty good business, although it takes a while to develop. Today, the main opportunity in this sector is in China and Indonesia. Anything made in the United States can be made in those countries at a fraction of the cost.

But getting your hands on good, inexpensive products is only the beginning. The tough part of wholesale is building a customer base. And, unfortunately, as your customers' businesses grow, they will eventually realize that they can cut you out and get their merchandise directly from the source.

The secret, here, is to develop unique products that only you can provide. You won't be able to do this right off the bat—but if you can move in this direction, you can be very successful as a wholesaler.

Then There's My Favorite Business . . .

My favorite type of business is what I'm calling "manufacturing." And in that general category, I include all sorts of things that aren't normally considered to be manufacturing businesses. I include, for example, publishing and the selling of private-label nutritional products. Manufacturing, to me, is any industry where you create the product and sell it directly to the end user.

I love this type of business, because it gives you complete control over the entire process, from inventing the product to closing the sale and even going back to the customer for more sales.

In the age of the Internet and globalization, manufacturing is a great business to be in. To create your product, you can use anyone the world over. And you can sell to the entire world, too.

takes is the discipline to set long-term goals for yourself and establish a realistic system to achieve them.

The best way I know to do that is to use the *ETR* goal-setting protocol. I've tried dozens of other methods, but nothing beats it. In a nutshell, you break your long-term goals into specific yearly, monthly, and weekly goals. Using those objectives as your guide, you create a daily to-do list. Then you prioritize the tasks on that list, making your number one priority for the day something that will take you one step closer to your primary long-term objective.

If you're reading this book, I'm assuming your primary objective is to achieve financial independence in no more than seven years. A logical stepping stone to that goal would be to start your own business within the next year. Using the *ETR* goal-setting protocol, you would determine what you need to accomplish every month to get that business started. You would break those monthly objectives into weekly objectives. And then you would prioritize your daily task lists.

Your number one priority for the day might be, for example, to do an hour's worth of Internet research about an idea you have for your new business . . . or to make arrangements to attend an upcoming trade show . . . or to contact three people that you'd like to add to your support network.

Get that one task done first thing in the morning, before you do anything else, and you'll kick-start your day with a great sense of accomplishment.

HOW TO FIND (AND TAKE ADVANTAGE OF) A GREAT MENTOR

It can take decades to build a career or a business. But, like Brad, you can shorten your learning curve—even drastically curtail it—with the help of a mentor.

With the advice, expertise, and support of an experienced person in your field, you can avoid the most common mistakes you are likely to make . . . overcome the stickiest problems . . . and find a shortcut to success.

WHAT CAN YOU LEARN FROM A MENTOR?

Surveys indicate that business leaders who had been mentored feel the experience was invaluable. They've said their mentors helped them build all kinds of skills, including decision making, strategic thinking, planning, coaching, and effectively managing others.

Earlier in this book, I briefly mentioned a few of my mentors. I learned priceless lessons about business from each of them.

From Perry, my first post-college boss, I learned the importance of dogged determination. Remember the story I told in Chapter 2 about Perry pushing me to call a Honda dealer over and over and over again, until they agreed to replace my engine? I didn't feel good about getting something we didn't deserve, but I never forgot that lesson in persistence.

From John, my second major mentor, I learned a great deal. The first lesson he taught me—by firing the woman who wanted to get me fired—was that a good leader needs to surround himself with the strongest people he can find. Another lesson had to do with the fundamental nature of business. "Until you make a sale," John explained patiently, "nothing else happens."

From Adam*, a client, partner, and part-time mentor, I discovered—relatively late in my career—two business secrets that have made me a better leader. For one thing, I no longer feel compelled to solve every problem put at my feet. I've watched Adam ignore countless squabbles and come out much the better for it. Before getting involved in a dispute these days,

I ask myself, "Can these people eventually come up with a satisfactory solution themselves?" If the answer is affirmative, I do nothing.

Thanks to Adam, I'm also now a huge believer in product quality. Having mastered the art of selling through my relationship with John, I tended to underestimate the importance of the product. I was one of those marketers who actually wanted to sell snow to Eskimos. In working with Adam, whose sole focus is always on quality, I've seen how much better a business becomes when that's what you concentrate on.

Chances are, you have no idea what you need to know to make the next leap forward in your career. But someone who's been there and done it before does. Getting the help of that person will make a very big difference in your future.

HOW TO FIND YOUR MENTOR

Look around your industry to find five successful business leaders who retired within the past two to five years. This two-to-five-year timeframe is important. If they've been retired any longer, they could be out of touch. Any sooner, and they're not yet bored enough with retirement to miss thinking about work.

Write each of these five people a short letter expressing genuine admiration for their careers. Compliment them on specific achievements. Then ask for advice on your own career.

Offer an invitation to go to lunch. Or, if they're located out of your local area, ask for a 15-minute phone call. And don't—I repeat, don't—offer them any compensation for their help . . . yet. Odds are, at least one of the five will respond positively to your invitation. If you find that you get along, you've got yourself a mentor.

Once you've found your mentor, make a list of the goals you want to work on. What do you want out of the relationship? What do you feel you need to learn? What can this person best teach you?

How to Make Sure You've Got a Good Mentor

A mentorship is a relationship built on learning. Your mentor should be your learning coach—someone you can talk to and trust. A good mentor should provide you with advice, feedback, and support. She should help you focus on your goals and give you direction that helps you succeed more quickly than you could alone.

A good mentor should help you learn the secrets to success in your field. (That's why finding one in your industry is so important.)

Your mentor should offer advice on skills she's found valuable. She should counsel you concerning various opportunities in your industry and different paths to success.

A good mentor won't tell you how to do your job. He should give you feedback and share his personal experiences, but not inundate you with lots of unsolicited advice. And a good mentor shouldn't be making decisions for you that you could make yourself. "Your mentor is not a savior," pointed out an article in *Black Enterprise*.

I agree. If you're going to learn from your mentor, he can't come up with every single solution for you . . . nor should you expect him to. Your mentor should act as a sounding board and as a trusted advisor and counselor. I like the way business writer Ron Yudd put it: "[Mentors] hold the flashlight so others can see the path."

Respect the Mentor-Mentee Relationship

To maintain your relationship with your mentor, you must recognize her value and reward her for it. Keep in mind that the kind of advice she is giving you is likely to have the most profound effect on your career. Although you can't measure the financial value of any specific suggestion ("Stop spending so much time on this fulfillment project. Get to work on improving your advertising."), you can bet that in the long run the effect will be very significant.

Show him you appreciate what he is doing for you. Tell him, in specific terms, what you have learned from him and thank him every time he meets with you. The psychological reward of knowing he is helping you succeed is his primary incentive. But that said, the time has now come to offer to compensate him for his time with money.

How much? That's up to you. Pay no more than you feel comfortable with and no less than your mentor thinks is fair. If you can't find a number in between those two figures, find another mentor.

One of my current mentors gets a check of several thousand dollars every time I spend time with him. On a per-hour basis, he's extremely well paid. But for the help he gives me in making key leadership and wealth-building decisions, the $30,000 to $40,000 a year I invest in him is a bargain.

If one mentor is valuable, multiple mentors can prove to be *invaluable*. This makes enormous sense when you consider it. It gives you not only the wisdom of one person who has been successfully doing what he's doing for years and years, but also the perspective of comparing the ideas and judgments of several experts.

Adopting a mentor or mentors requires a temporary abnegation of pride. Or perhaps something beyond that—the wisdom to understand that one's own ideas are not always the best ideas.

HOW TO PROVE YOURSELF IN THE MARKETPLACE

Brad built his business by consistently delivering high-quality service. In addition, he established a reputation with his clients as being reliable, punctual, and hardworking—and it paid off. As a result, they not only continued to do business with him, they also recommended him to many other people.

No matter what you're selling—a product or a service—a satisfied customer is one of your most valuable business-building tools. So here's what you have to do:

- *First and most important, focus on quality.* Does your service meet or exceed the promises made in your ad? Does your product look like it's worth even more than what the customer paid for it? If your products/services are—and continue to be—top shelf, you will have no trouble keeping your customers happy and getting repeat business.
- *Pamper your customers.* The more and better attention you give them, the more responsive they will be to your future offers. Generally speaking, if you know your customer you know what she wants. And if you can give her that—in greater quantities and higher quality—she'll stick with you. My own experience confirms this. The businesses I work with that provide better-than-ordinary products and customer service enjoy higher retention rates and greater back-end sales.

- *Remember that your top priority is to provide products and/or services to your customers.* It is the customer who, ultimately, pays your wages. Toward that end, your main job is to make the customer happy.

  When we say, "The customer is always right," we aren't naïve enough to think that this is literally true. There are many times when a customer may be uninformed, out of line, unrealistic, or downright unpleasant. What we mean is that in any transaction, the end result must please the customer. So if, for example, the customer wants a refund—even if it's not justified—give it without an argument.

- *Always overdeliver.* This means not only consistently doing what you promise to do but also going above and beyond good service—going out of your way to make your customer happy by recommending an alternate or supplemental product . . . fixing a problem on a weekend or holiday . . . or doing a small service for free.

  Real estate developer Frank McKinney earmarks a portion of his profits for "relationship building." On every estate home he builds, he will usually fix any problem the client brings to his attention, even if it is not covered by the standard one-year warranty. He credits this "extraordinary" approach to exceeding customer expectations as part of his phenomenal success.

- *Customer service and sales should go hand-in-hand.* Most businesses divide themselves in half. On the one side, you have sales and marketing. On the other side, fulfillment and customer service. Often these activities are separated physically, with separate management, separate work philosophies, and separate personnel. Big mistake.

  Good salespeople already know the benefits of providing superior service to their customers—but it's equally beneficial to a business to have customer service people trained in sales. Picture this: a customer calls in with a problem or a question. But instead of simply handling the problem or answering the question, your CS rep persuades this already satisfied customer to buy your weekly "special" or sign up for another year of your service.

HOW TO GROW YOUR ROLODEX

Brad developed a network of successful, well-connected contacts that were a tremendous help to him. But there's more to building a support network than introducing yourself—or being introduced—to the right people. When you meet them, you have to get them to like you.

From *The Power of Charm: How to Win Anyone Over in Any Situation* (AMACOM, 2006), by Brian Tracy and Ron Arden, here are five ways to charm the people you hope to include in your network:

- *Show acceptance.* "The greatest gift you can give other people," Arden and Tracy say, "is the attitude of unconditional positive regard." And even if you aren't fortunate enough to be surrounded by people to whom you can muster unconditional regard (let's face it—such people are rare), you can nevertheless exude a lot of charm simply by letting the other person know that, although there may be points at which you fail to agree, your fundamental opinion of them is positive. The best way to show acceptance, Tracy and Arden say, is to smile. "When you smile with happiness at seeing people, their self-esteem jumps automatically. They feel happy about themselves. They feel important and valuable."
- *Show admiration.* After you've warmed up your charm victim by giving him that accepting smile, boost his self-esteem by telling him that you admire him. Everyone likes a compliment—even a false one—but it is much better (and more charming) if you can identify in your target some characteristic or quality that you genuinely admire. Almost everyone has something that can be admired, even if it is as innocuous as his posture or her tone of voice. Before you voice your admiration, internalize it—in other words, convince yourself that you do, indeed, admire that quality. A sincere compliment is a hundred times more powerful than a faked one.
- *Show approval.* "Throughout life, all humans have a deep unconscious need for approval of their actions and accomplishments," Tracy and Arden say. People never grow tired of compliments so

long as they are sincere. When somebody does something well or good, let him or her know that you noticed. Showing approval for specific behavior is the best way to ensure that it will happen again. As with showing admiration, showing approval is best when it is sincere—and that usually means paying attention to specifics. (As in, "I really liked the way you collated that report, John.")

- *Show appreciation.* When someone does something nice for you—big or small—say "thank you." Saying thanks is more than merely uttering the words, Tracy and Arden remind us. It's about making eye contact and showing true appreciation by your tone of voice.
- *Give attention.* This is the most important arrow in the charmer's quiver. "When you pay close attention to other people," Tracy and Arden say, "the more valuable and important they will feel they are, and the more they will like you."

Exhibiting these qualities is easier and more effective when you develop certain skills:

- *Be a charming listener.*
  - Listen attentively. (Turn off that television. Put down that paper.)
  - Pause for a moment before replying. (This indicates that you are giving the other person's comments due consideration.)
  - Ask questions when you need clarification.
  - Paraphrase complicated or convoluted speeches before replying to them.
- *Be an attentive listener.*
  - Face the person you are talking to.
  - Make direct eye contact.
  - Move your gaze from one to another of the speaker's eyes as he or she is talking.
  - Nod appropriately.
  - Provide verbal clues that you are interested in the conversation ("Yes, I see what you mean").
  - Tilt your head occasionally.
- *Be quick to smile, laugh, and provide compliments whenever it is*

appropriate. This may take practice at first, but with repetition it can become a habit. The bonus for you is that you will feel happier.

- *Act—as much and as frequently as you can—as if you really, really like the other person.*

PARTNERS AND SUPERSTARS—HOW TO FIND AND WORK WITH THE RIGHT PEOPLE

Brad's income potential took a giant leap forward when he hired Tom, a superstar employee who was eventually able to take over the day-to-day operations of the company and leave Brad free to explore other opportunities. It took another leap forward when he partnered with Will to start a new business.

Here are some tips to help you build your future with the right people:

- A really great partner (or key employee) is someone who has the potential to take the long voyage with you. Ask yourself, "This person may be fine now, but will he be able to do a great job when the business is 10 times this size?" If you can't answer affirmatively, look for someone else.
- When you hire or partner with someone, she should understand that your commitment is to a particular vision. If you can inspire her to commit to that vision, too, it will be much easier for you to work together and make the right business-building decisions.
- Think about your own strengths. And then think about your weaknesses. Does your partner (or key employee) have qualities that complement yours? Can he take up the slack you leave?
- Make sure the business is always involved in providing a product or service that you both like . . . or don't do it.
- And make sure you both agree on the way you would handle hypothetical situations that could affect the business—what you and your partner would do, for example, if one of you wanted out.

HOW TO DEVELOP A SECOND STREAM OF INCOME

You can get yourself closer to your ultimate goal of financial independence within seven years by using the talents and skills you are already developing to start a side business and add a second stream of income to your bank account.

I'm a chicken entrepreneur, so I don't recommend doing what Brad did—which was to quit his $49,000 a year accounting job and start a brand-new business he knew little about. Because Brad made so many good decisions, he was able to succeed despite his brash leap into unknown territory. But that won't work for everybody.

Instead, I suggest that you start small and build gradually. This limits your risk in case your new business fails (as many do). For instance, Alan Silver, whom you read about in Chapter 5, waited until his vitamin company was profitable before he gave up his steady income as an office-supply salesman.

At some point in the future, you may realize that you are making more money from your second income than you are from the first. At that point, you may choose to drop your "day job."

I've seen this happen dozens of times. In some cases, that second stream of income turns into a river . . . and then a tidal wave.

SHOOTING FOR AN EXTRA $25,000 A YEAR IS A GOOD— AND REASONABLE—PLACE TO START

There are all sorts of ways to supplement your income by $25,000 a year. There are as many ways as there are businesses. You can increase your income by selling your services to the company you work for— going freelance. You can also add a second stream of income by selling your services to other firms while you're still working for your current employer. (Noncompetitive firms. You don't want to do anything you could get fired for.)

If you have a financially valued skill, you can expect to earn between $100 and $500 an hour. At $100 an hour, you would have to work 250 hours—an extra five hours a week—to make $25,000. At $500 an hour, it would take you only about an hour a week to earn $25,000.

If you would rather supplement your income by trying out a different financially valued skill, consider becoming an advertising copywriter, graphic designer, or any of the dozens of other freelance professions that cater to the direct-marketing industry.

A GOOD WAY TO CREATE A SECOND INCOME IS TO START A PART-TIME LOCAL SERVICE BUSINESS

It doesn't take much to start a part-time, local service business. If you don't have time to do the actual work yourself (as a handyman, housecleaner, landscaper, etc.), hire a friend or relative. At first, you'll make little more than what you pay your "employee." For example, you might collect $15 an hour but you'll have to pay him or her $10.

A friend of mine began by sending out postcards advertising her housecleaning service. She mailed 200 postcards to addresses in an affluent community and received 11 positive responses. That yielded the equivalent of two-and-a-half full-time jobs, so she hired her cousin and two friends. My friend was making less than $25 a week per worker, but she was into a business that could be gradually expanded into something substantial.

Another acquaintance of mine started a lawn-care business this way and now has more than 200 accounts. He's already quit his job to devote his full-time energies to managing what he expects will one day be a million-dollar company.

Chances are, you won't turn a little business like this into a fortune. But if it brings you an extra $5,000 or $10,000 a year . . . that can add up.

GETTING STARTED IN THE SERVICE BUSINESS—RIGHT AWAY

As I said before, the best thing about going into a service business is that it's relatively easy to get into and then expand into something much bigger:

- Identify a market where service providers make (or can make) a lot of money.

- Find out as much as you can about how they do their business.
- If possible, subcontract or work as an employee for one of them.
- When you've learned enough to provide good or excellent service yourself, find a marketing niche—and start looking for customers.
- Figure out how to attract new customers—first and foremost—and keep doing it until you master it. Then do it some more.
- As your business grows, focus on quality and excellent customer service.

Get started, today . . . and you could be on your way to seven figures.

PART III

WHY YOU MUST ACT NOW

If you've read the previous chapters, you've learned a lot about what it takes to get rich quickly. There is more to learn, to be sure—but if you are motivated, you have more than enough information to begin building your own seven-figure net worth.

Now, in Part III, you will learn why it is imperative for you to start your wealth-building program as soon as possible.

If you have ever set a goal and failed to achieve it, this section is for you.

CHAPTER 11

THE BABY BOOMER CHALLENGE

WHY 50- AND 60-YEAR-OLDS MUST FOLLOW THE SEVEN YEARS TO SEVEN FIGURES PLAN

On January 1, 2006—the day I started writing this book—Kathleen Casey-Kirschling turned 60.

Who is Kathleen Casey-Kirschling? According to the record books, she is the first of my generation, the first baby born in 1946 and, therefore, the first baby boomer.

In the newspapers that morning, there were several articles about her. All of them had the same angle: what are the baby boomers thinking about now? And the answers were the same: we are thinking about retirement.

Ah, retirement! That lovely notion! Living comfortably without toil, without stress, without working! Who could resist such an idea?

Not me, nor my contemporaries. Not even our parents. But before the turn of the 20th century, before the advent of the modern city with its population migrations and proliferation of factories and office buildings, retirement didn't exist.

In the pre-industrial days, you worked until you dropped. As you aged, you did less of the hardest work, but you worked. This is still the rule in many agrarian cultures. Old people stay in the family circle (usually as respected elders) until, surrounded by their children and grandchildren, they curl up and die.

THE BOOMERS TURN 60

Born one second after midnight on January 1, 1946, the *Philadelphia Inquirer* heralded Kathleen Casey-Kirschling as the first child born to the post-World War II generation. Later that same year, it's interesting to note, George Bush, Jr. and Bill Clinton were also born.

During the month that preceded her 60th birthday, Kathleen was the subject of numerous magazine and newspaper stories, as well as segments on a number of national television shows, including NBC's *Today* show and the *CBS Evening News*.

"Turning 60 is monumental because of all the issues facing healthcare and Social Security and nursing homes," she told *USA Today*. " And I don't like the way the country is going right now."

Things are much different now. We move away from our families as soon as we are able. We depend on ourselves. And when our parents become old and feeble, we put them in state or private wards with other people's parents so they will not burden us.

When the farm was the primary source of income, our lives were closely connected to the land . . . to the seasons and the weather. We accepted life and death as a natural cycle—like the life and death of plants—and lived accordingly. When the factory replaced the farm as our primary income source, things changed—including our view of ourselves. We began to live and die like replaceable machine parts.

Industrialization changed the way we worked. No longer did the sun, rain, and snow dictate our hours. In modern times, thanks to modern inventions, we can work around the clock, six or seven days a week.

Ah, yes. Things have gotten better.

We don't have to wash dishes by hand anymore. And we don't have to work until the day we die. When we are lucky enough to reach an age where our company no longer wants us (when we become too slow, too set in our ways, and/or too expensive), we can retire. We can just stop working and take up fishing. Or golf. Or knitting. Whatever we want, really. Thanks to the benevolence of our employer and our government, we have the money and the time to really enjoy ourselves.

That was the idea of retirement. And for a while, at least, it seemed to be working.

For a period of about two generations—from the end of World War I until the 1970s—most American factory and office workers could expect to live reasonably well in retirement on the financial benefits they had been promised.

But, alas, that has changed. For baby boomers like Kathleen Casey-Kirschling and me, the promise of being able to pass our post-working years at leisure has been broken.

WORRIED ABOUT RETIREMENT? YOU ARE NOT ALONE

There are about 80 million baby boomer Americans (born between 1946 and 1964) who have inherited the dream of retirement. And most of them are coming to recognize that the dream may not come true.

According to the *MetLife Survey of American Attitudes Toward Retirement: What's Changed?* (www.metlife.com), baby boomers are "increasingly anxious" about how they will support themselves during their post-working lives.

And with good reason.

The "three pillars" of retirement security—Social Security, Medicare, and private pensions—are crumbling and in danger of collapsing.

Social Security: Government's Biggest Promise

The monthly Social Security checks that used to cover our basic needs—housing, utilities, and food—are inadequate today.

According to the Social Security Administration (www.ssa.gov), a typical retiree in 2005 received a monthly benefit of $1,002. With this amount of money, most people wouldn't be able to pay for much beyond rent (which averaged $940 in 2005, according to a survey by real estate data firm M/PF Yieldstar reported by MSN's Melinda Fulmer).

And even those who are fortunate to live in a home that is completely paid for would be $73.25 *in the hole* after paying for groceries (at an average of $92 a week, according to a Food Marketing Institute study), utilities (at an average of $234.25 per month in 2003, according to a U.S. Bureau of Labor and Statistics Consumer Expenditures report), and operating expenses for a small car ($473 a month, assuming the car is driven 10,000 miles annually, according to a 2004 report from the American Automobile Association and Runzheimer International).

And the trend is moving in the wrong direction.

Until now, the amount of money drawn into the Treasury from Social Security taxes (which show on your pay stub as money withheld for FICA and Medicare) has exceeded the outgoing payments made by the SSA for these programs. But according to the Government Accountability Office, the SSA will be paying out more in benefits than it collects by 2017. And by 2041, all of its funds will be depleted.

Needless to say, the younger you are now, the less you can expect to see in Social Security benefits. So the bottom line is this: if you are expecting the government to take care of your basic necessities (i.e., rent, utilities, and food), you'll be bitterly disappointed. Rely on Social Security for your retirement years, and you can plan on living in a rented room and eating dog food.

What about Medicare?

For baby boomers, health expenses are going to become an increasingly large part of their personal budgets. Baby boomers aged 50 to 64 already spend twice as much on health-related expenses than younger adults.

And it keeps getting worse. The average remaining-life expectancy for 65-year-olds is about 18.2 years, up from 13.9 years in 1950—and it continues to increase. This means that more people will be drawing from the same rapidly emptying pool of benefits.

Worse yet, the medical coverage that Medicare was once able to provide to Americans will be unavailable in the future. Before most baby boomers hit 65, in fact, this government program may be taking care of nothing more than basic medication. According to the American Association of Retired Persons, "Medicare provides limited coverage of certain healthcare services, including mental health, long-term care, vision, hearing, and dental care. In addition, while the Medicare prescription drug benefit is a strong first step toward affordable drug coverage for people on Medicare, the benefit leaves a significant coverage gap that must be filled."

And, of course, healthcare costs keep rising. In a May 2005 article in the *Annals of Internal Medicine,* Thomas Bodenheimer, M.D., explains that U.S. healthcare expenditures have risen a staggering 40 percent since 1988—and he speculates that they will rise to $3.6 trillion by 2013.

This steady escalation in expenses means that as the size of your Social Security checks diminishes, you'll be paying even more for your out-of-pocket medical needs.

Private Pension Funds Are in Terrible Shape, Too

And if you're counting on income from a pension to fund your retirement, you might be out of luck.

The Pension Benefit Guaranty Corporation (PBGC) is a quasi-governmental agency that insures the pensions of 44 million American workers. The organization slipped into a deficit in 2002 after rescuing failed pension plans in the steel industry. Then came bankrupt airlines and utilities, swelling its deficit to more than $23 billion in 2004.

Aggravating the situation is the fact that U.S. companies are underfunded on their pensions to the tune of $450 billion. At a November 2004 forum titled "PBGC Financial Woes," Doug Elliott, president of the Center on Federal Financial Institutions, said that the organization has about 15 years left before it runs out of funds.

According to Bradley Belt, executive director of the PBGC, there are only three possible "solutions" to the current crisis:

- Corporations will have to start kicking in substantially higher premiums just to pay off current obligations.
- The U.S. government will have to come in and bail out the system.
- Pension funds will be reduced.

All three solutions are forms of thievery. The money that was paid into the system should have been enough to take care of the payouts. But something went awry.

The popular explanation is that the recent rapid decline in pension funding is the result of a combination of an eroding stock market coupled with low interest rates. (Lower interest rates make long-term obligations seem larger.) But there are other factors at play, too, such as globalization and airline deregulation.

The PBGC has taken over 291 pension plans in the steel and metals industry since 1975. It estimates that it faces about $40 billion in liabilities in the manufacturing sector and another $33 billion in airlines and other transportation companies, telecom, and utilities. "It will affect everybody who has a defined-benefit plan," says Rania Sedhom, a lawyer who specializes in employee benefits.

Of course, the officials and experts who are telling us "there is no need to panic" are the same people who are admitting to how bad things are.

WHAT ABOUT THE AMERICAN ECONOMY?

The American economy is large and dynamic, and, therefore, capable of almost unlimited growth. Still, the macroeconomic outlook for baby boomers looks stark. Our pensions have shrunk, our savings have all but disappeared, and there is plenty of evidence that the government is making matters worse. The dream of retiring at 65 and spending the next 20 years "on vacation" has been replaced with the dread of slipping into poverty.

Politicians, academics, economists, and authors will try to figure out big-picture solutions. But while they are doing so, baby boomers should make plans—personal plans—that are not dependent on Social Security, Medicare, and private pensions.

I am not saying these three pillars of retirement will completely collapse. I'm saying they might.

And even if these beleaguered institutions somehow manage to provide some financial assistance to the 80 million Americans of the baby boomer generation, they won't be able to do nearly what they've promised.

Which means that if you want to have any chance of retiring, you are going to have to create your own wealth.

That's what this book is about: creating your own wealth. And the particular ideas, techniques, and strategies I've talked about in the previous chapters are especially useful to baby boomers who don't have 30 or 40 years to get rich slowly. They are all aimed at achieving a seven-figure net worth in seven years or less.

The stories you've been reading are full of practical ways to do just that—and they have all worked for the people involved. If you are a baby boomer who wants to enjoy the dream of retirement, or if you are a younger person who is simply eager to get rich in the shortest possible time, you could do worse than to follow some of those very good examples.

CHAPTER 12

LESSONS FROM
LIFE: WHAT I'VE
LEARNED ABOUT
BUILDING WEALTH
QUICKLY

In answering the challenge of this book's title—how to acquire a seven-figure net worth in seven years or less—I made sure to follow a few rules:

- I would start with a blank slate.
- I would be critical of the premise.
- I would stick to what I know to be true.
- I would "show" rather than "tell."

And, finally, I would admit my shortcomings.

These rules weren't created randomly. They were suggested by what I learned from writing my three previous books on success: *Automatic Wealth*, *Power & Persuasion*, and *Automatic Wealth for Grads . . . and Anyone Else Just Starting Out*.

In my enthusiasm to tell people what I know, I can be too self-assured and too critical and dismissive of contrary ideas. I so strongly believe in my way of doing things (particularly when it comes to wealth building) that I have sometimes pooh-poohed other strategies without giving them a fair shake.

When I agreed to write this book, I promised myself that I wouldn't do that. I began by erasing from the blackboard of my mind any pre-existing notations about "good" and "bad" ways to get rich.

STARTING WITH A TABULA RASA

"Maybe you can get rich quickly by trading stocks," I told myself. "And maybe options and commodities and currencies can work, too. Maybe you can even acquire a seven-figure net worth in seven years by tapping into the power of positive thinking."

So I wiped away the cynicism I had for those wealth gurus whose ideas about getting rich had previously seemed so hokey to me.

Beginning with a blank slate, I gave my writing assistant a list of a dozen of my friends and colleagues who had made lots of money quickly—and I told her to ask them how they did it.

"Just write down what they say," I said. "Even if it contradicts what I've been preaching in *Early to Rise* (my e-zine)."

If she discovered that someone had gotten rich by investing in options, good! If she found someone for whom oil and gas leases were the answer, we'd tell his story! "Let the chips fall where they may," I announced boldly.

As you know from reading the book, we ended up with eight fascinating stories about eight interesting people who made their fortunes in different ways. But we found some recurring patterns:

- They all earned high incomes.
- They all had equity in a business.
- Most of them invested in real estate.

These patterns—it seems to me—are the core of this book. If you can understand them and incorporate them into your life, there's no reason why you shouldn't be able to repeat the successes of these eight people.

Whatever you do . . . however you choose to go about building your own wealth . . . I wish you luck. I hope I have convinced you that becoming a high-income, high-net-worth, independent business-person might not be as tough as it seems. And I hope that the stories

I've recounted for you in these pages will help you on your path, even if only in some very small way.

THE LIFESTYLE YOU HAVE ALWAYS DREAMED OF . . .

Imagine this.

You wake up as the sun comes up, feeling refreshed and eager to start a new day. After 10 minutes of stretching, you shower and ride your bicycle to the office. There you sit down to a hot cup of coffee, turn on your computer, and punch up the daily receipts.

While you were sleeping, 160 new orders came in at $50 each ($8,000), along with eight back-end VIP orders at $1,250 each. That's a total of $18,000. Not bad.

Buoyed by the good news, you begin your morning's work by writing an article about your favorite topic. (Pets? Golf? Astronomy?) There are 8,000 people on your e-mail file who share your enthusiasm. They have all signed up to receive your free e-zine, and look forward to hearing from you every day.

For several years now, you have been writing to these people. Some days, you write just a few sentences—perhaps summarizing something interesting you read in the newspaper. Other days, you write a longer, more thoughtful piece about an idea you've been ruminating on for weeks.

You typically spend about 90 minutes writing. When you are done, you save the file and send it. A minute later, your readers have it in their in-boxes.

The rest of your morning is devoted to a meeting with your marketing director, who has been making back-end deals with other companies that sell products related to yours. He is largely responsible for that $18,000 worth of sales you woke up to, and is excited about some new deals he's signed.

At 11:30, your personal trainer arrives and puts you through a vigorous, 30-minute workout. You shower (your office has a shower and a gym), dress, and then meet an old friend for lunch at a local eatery.

After lunch, you do a little shopping and then wander over to the local museum to catch a new exhibit. You'll meet your sister later in the afternoon for an espresso at your favorite café, and you'll be home by 5:00 to spend the rest of the day at your leisure.

That doesn't sound so bad, does it?

Guess what? That is just the kind of workday you could have if you follow in the footsteps of the people I profiled for this book. At least half of them made their biggest money by starting a home-based, Internet-driven business.

Because of how huge the Internet is these days—with billions of people plugged in all over the world—it's possible to find an active, profitable market for almost any conceivable business. Pick *any* subject (chess, ballroom dancing, gourmet cooking) and there are active Internet communities reading and corresponding about it.

These are all potential buyers for your products. And when you make an initial sale to one of these core customers, you can add him to your database and sell to him over and over again.

Based on my personal experience consulting for dozens of Internet-based businesses, big and small, local and international, you can realistically expect to earn between $100 and $250 (and more) on every one of your core customers.

Let's do the math.

If each of your core customers is worth $100 (net), how many would you need to give yourself a $200,000 income?

Answer: 2,000.

And how long would it take you to acquire a database of 2,000 loyal customers?

Answer: my best guess would be six months to a year.

And if you did acquire 2,000 customers in one year, how many customers could you expect to have by the end of the second year?

Answer: between 6,000 and 10,000.

And if you did get 10,000 customers, how much would you be making from them?

Answer: a million bucks a year.

My own little Internet business, my *Early to Rise* e-zine, has about 160,000 core customers.

At least four of my colleagues have Internet-based businesses, all of them considerably bigger than *ETR*.

I know a martial arts expert whose Internet business is only five or six years old . . . and yet it is already a multimillion-dollar money machine.

Another friend recently set up a self-help-related Internet business. He has about 3,000 core customers and is adding 500 a month. He is already making a decent income from it. "Unless you really blow it," I told him, "you'll be making an extra hundred grand—at least—a year from now."

The Internet offers businesspeople the revolutionary opportunity to precisely target potential customers in the world's fastest-growing marketplace. There is no business I can think of that wouldn't benefit enormously from doing this as part of its marketing strategy.

The Internet also makes it possible for you to "talk" (meaning "sell") to your core customers on a regular basis for practically nothing.

Pick a topic—something you love. Make a marketing plan. Figure out what you can sell, relatively cheaply, to establish your base of core customers. Focus on selling first. Everything else will take care of itself in due time.

You will have to work hard the first year. Probably harder than you are used to. But don't worry. You'll be so excited by what you are doing, so motivated by the idea that you are making a business out of something you're passionate about, that you won't notice how many hours you are putting into your work.

At the end of 12 or 18 months, your new business should be in the black. At the end of year two, you should be banking a nice profit. In year three, if all goes as it should, your business will double. And it will double again in years four and five, and even in year six.

Some time before year seven, you will not only be rich enough to retire, you will also be enjoying the enviable life I previously described.

This book won't change the world. In fact, chances are it won't change you. Odds are, you will read it, put it aside, and then—sooner or later—forget about it.

It doesn't have to be that way, but—statistically speaking—that's what's probable.

Do you know what else is probable?

- That if you start a new diet, you'll be fatter next year than you are today.
- That if you try to quit smoking, you'll be back to a pack a day in two weeks.

- That if you try to replace *any bad habit* with *any good one*, you'll fail.

Those are the probabilities. But why should you be tethered to the *probabilities of failure*? Wouldn't it be better to be driven by the *possibility of success*?

Isn't it better to try and risk failure than to fail simply for fear of failing? And in trying, doesn't it make more sense to imitate the one or two—or eight—ways you can succeed than to ape the many ways you can't?

The question you need to ponder right now isn't, "Will *Seven Years to Seven Figures* work for everybody?" (Because the answer is surely "no.") But, instead, to consider, "Can it work for me?"

And the answer to that is . . . "maybe."

Maybe it will. Maybe it won't. It depends on how good I have been at identifying the patterns of wealth building and how applicable those patterns can be in your life.

And it also depends on you.

How do you intend to use this book?

Have you been reading it *critically*—to see how well its ideas match your own?

Have you been reading it *addictively*—to find passages that satisfy some psychological need you have to feel better or worse about yourself or to have or dismiss the hope of future wealth?

Have you been reading it *loyally*—because you have read my books before and you enjoy *Early to Rise* and you feel like a part of our little community?

Or have you been reading it *pragmatically*—to discover which of the habits, practices, and strategies that worked for others might also work for you?

And if you've been doing that—and if you have identified two, three, or four strategies for getting rich quickly . . . what will you do next?

The secret to success, Frank Lloyd Wright said, is "dedication, hard work, and an unremitting devotion to the things you want to see happen."

Getting wealthy is like getting skinny. We all want to do it, but few of us are willing to do what it takes.

So what does it take to get wealthy?

Three things:

- A plan of action.
- Making the time to follow the plan.
- The willpower to do the work.

Are you on your way to seven figures in seven years?
You have everything you need right now. So go for it!

AFTERWORD

Afterwords are not common features of books these days, and probably with good reason. They are a vestige of an earlier day in publishing, when some writers took a more leisurely approach and readers read at a more casual pace. Today, authors must compete with television and the Internet. We recognize that if we are lucky enough to find an audience, we must not try to hold on to them too long.

Also—to admit the truth—the Afterword was probably always a bad device. Having one indicates a certain weakness. Why hadn't the author said everything he or she meant to say in the previous chapters?

Still, I have always wanted to write an Afterword. And so I am writing this. But I will make it short. And I will justify it this way: if you read nothing else in this book, read this. In the next several paragraphs I will restate, succinctly, everything I have learned about building wealth quickly.

THE FIRST THING I KNOW ABOUT
BUILDING WEALTH QUICKLY

It is tempting to believe that if you could put your savings into the right vehicle—stocks, commodities, limited partnerships—wealth would follow. But it is almost impossible to acquire a great deal of wealth in a very short time by investing your money passively.

The lure of this method of getting rich is enormous, because it appeals to one of our most fundamentally human instincts—laziness. Do one thing. Do it right. And then sit back and watch the money flow in.

I call laziness an instinct, rather than a fault, because it informs almost every activity we engage in. We all want to find easier ways of accomplishing valuable objectives. To get more by working less.

This instinct helps us become better students (by discovering more efficient study techniques), better businesspeople (by finding more efficient production techniques), better marketers (by learning more efficient sales techniques), and better parents (by seeking out more efficient child-rearing strategies).

But laziness is a two-edged sword. If we allow our natural efficiency impulse to impel us to neglect the necessary work that must be done, we will—quickly or slowly, but almost always—fail in the long run.

When it comes to accomplishing our financial goals, we must use our laziness to work efficiently . . . but we must still work.

Passive investing does not take much effort. You read about some investment advisor who made a fortune in the past and you figure, "If he can do that with my money, I'll be on Easy Street."

But, as the Securities and Exchange Commission so often reminds us, past performance is no indication of future success.

I am not saying that you can't make good money with things like stocks or options. I am saying that to do so you will have to work hard. You will need a very good system and you will have to do an enormous amount of research—and you will have to revise and update both your research and your system on a daily basis. In short, to make a ton of money with passive investments, you will have to become very active about them.

I have invested passively for more than 20 years. And in that time I have done about as well as the next guy—which is to say, not very well. Yes, I have my stories. But for every 50 percent or 100 percent return on investment (ROI) I've had in the passive markets, I have suffered half a dozen breakevens or losses.

The successful stock investors and investment advisors I know (and, having been in the investment publishing business for 25 years, I know a few) have achieved their success by working very, very hard.

So that's the first important idea this book was meant to convey: if you want to create a seven-figure net worth in seven years (or less), you will have to choose a wealth-building method that involves a good deal of hard work.

THE SECOND THING I KNOW

The single most effective way to become wealthy fast is to dramatically increase your income. There are several ways to do that, some of which have been explained in Part 2 of this book. Basically, I'm talking about increasing your income in at least one of three ways:

1. Do what you are currently doing for a living . . . but do it better.
2. Develop a financially valued skill. I have shown what I mean by a "financially valued skill" many times in this book. I have also explained it in detail in two of my past books on wealth building, *Automatic Wealth* and *Automatic Wealth for Grads . . . and Anyone Else Just Starting Out*. I cannot overemphasize the importance of this objective. Essentially, it means getting yourself in a position where you directly affect your company's bottom line—which usually has something to do with sales or marketing. Learning how to effectively sell your company's products is a necessity if you want to get big promotions, big salary increases, and big profit incentives. (You should also learn how to sell yourself.)
3. Augment your income. Most of the wealth builders profiled in Part 2 of this book were not satisfied with a single source of income. They realized that they could make far more money by *reinvesting* their knowledge and skills outside of their primary source of income. Some of the opportunities they took advantage of involved consulting. Some involved starting secondary or even tertiary businesses.

That's the second thing I know about becoming wealthy fast. And it relates to the first thing, because all the ways to dramatically increase your income involve hard work.

THE THIRD THING I KNOW

A high income alone is usually not sufficient to provide you with a seven-figure net worth in seven years. To achieve that lofty objective, you have to get a better-than-average return on your investments.

Again, you can't do that by simply picking the "right" stock and sitting back. You have to find the right investment vehicle . . . and then you have to *work* it.

By "work it," I mean work hard on it. You must learn exactly how that investment appreciates. If it's a business you are investing in, you must learn how that business sells its products and how it generates profits. Neither of these things will be easy to find out, for they are, in effect, the closely guarded secrets of that business.

However, if you follow the strategies used by the people profiled in Part 2 of this book, you will be able to acquire this valuable knowledge in a relatively short time. A year or two of serious investigation should do the trick.

Once you have acquired that knowledge, you must put it to work. You must use what you have discovered to sell more products at higher prices to an increasingly large number of customers.

In my experience, and in the experience of most of the people profiled in this book, there are three investments you can make—of time and/or money—that will allow you to *work* them:

1. You can invest in the business that employs you by getting a profit-sharing compensation package.
2. You can invest in another business—either one that a friend or family member runs or one you run yourself in the evening and on weekends.
3. You can invest in real estate.

These three investment vehicles can give you an extraordinary ROI . . . if and only if you *work* them. It is not enough to make the investment. You have to use your financially valued skills (especially your understanding of marketing) to make them grow and become more profitable.

It is only by making—actively making—your investments more profitable that you can reasonably expect to enjoy the extraordinary returns that—combined with earning a much higher income—will enable you to achieve a seven-figure net worth in seven years.

Nature designed us with two instincts toward work. One is to avoid it. And the other is to relish it. The stories and advice in this book are meant to help you figure out how to do that. It won't be easy . . . but it can be done.

I'll leave you with one more thought . . .

If we publish a revised edition of this book several years from now—and I hope we will—it would be nice to replace Part 2 with eight new stories.

If you get started now, yours could be one of them.

INDEX